Spicy VEGETARIAN FEASTS

Add the magic of spices to your cooking
and make every meal a treat.

Inside front cover:
Rich Saffron Soup
Meatless Chilli

Inside back cover:
Gingered Carrots
Spicy Okra and Tomato Sauté
Mexican Rice Salad

Spicy
VEGETARIAN FEASTS

Gourmet Recipes Full of Flavour and Alluringly Aromatic

by

Martha Rose Shulman

Illustrated by Elaine Hill

THORSONS PUBLISHING GROUP
Wellingborough, Northamptonshire
Rochester, Vermont

Published in the UK by Thorsons Publishers Ltd., Denington Estate, Wellingborough, Northamptonshire NN8 2RQ, and in the USA by Thorsons Publishers Inc., 377 Park Avenue South, New York, NY10016. Thorsons Publishers Inc. are distributed to the trade by Inner Traditions International Ltd., New York.

First published May 1986
Second Impression October 1986

Library of Congress Cataloging-in-Publication Data

Shulman, Martha Rose.
  Spicy vegetarian feasts.

  Inciudes index.
  1. Cookery (Herbs)   2. Spices.
  3. Vegetarian cookery.
  I. Title
TX819.H4S59 1986   641.6'383   86-1409

ISBN 0-7225-1220-1 (pbk.)

British Library Cataloguing in Publication Data

Shulman, Martha Rose
  Spicy vegetarian feasts: gourmet recipes
  full of flavour and alluringly aromatic.
  1. Vegetarian cookery
  I. Title
  641.5'636   TX837

  ISBN 0-7225-1220-1

Printed and bound in Great Britain by
Whitstable Litho Ltd., Whitstable, Kent

Contents

In memory of my mother, Carol Rees Shulman.

Acknowledgements

While researching this book I had the pleasure of reading Julie Sahni's marvellous *Classic Indian Cooking* (William Morrow and Company, 1980), and I feel forever indebted to Mrs. Sahni, not only a wonderful cook but a captivating writer, for helping me understand the rich and varied cuisine of that huge country. In so doing she has also taught me much about the country itself (and given me a good dose of the travel bug to go there).

I am equally grateful to Madhur Jaffrey, whose seemingly endless collections *Eastern Vegetarian Cooking* (Jonathan Cape, London 1983), *World of the East Vegetarian Cooking* Alfred A. Knopf, New York, 1981, not only increased my desire to visit India but also every other Asian country. Both of these cooks, as well as Elizabeth David, have been an inspiration.

I am *most* grateful to my close friend and efficient assistant, Laurie Dill, who helped me with much of the editorial work and carefully tested almost all of the recipes in this book. Laurie is a great cook in her own right, and her suggestions for improvements on many of the recipes have been invaluable.

Foreword

It is very frustrating to write a short book on spice cookery as I have done here. Once I began my research I wanted to delve deeply into every cuisine, for spices are in use all over the world—they are the ingredients that give many cuisines their special characters. It is often through the use of spices that cooks have given their personal stamp to their recipes, and I would have liked to experiment to the hilt with my own, to research and cook with those of others to a greater extent, to embark upon the same kind of voyage that brought fifteenth- and sixteenth-century explorers to new continents in search of these very seasonings.

Space and time have not allowed me to do this. What I hope to provide you with here is a small collection of recipes that will familiarize you with spices you may never have used before and broaden your repertoire if you are acquainted with these fragrant, magic ingredients. It is an attempt to make the world of cookery a little smaller, to bring a little of India, China, Mexico, Southeast Asia, the Middle East, as well as Europe and the United States, together in your kitchen.

Introduction

"... Who knows which palaces, now crumbling to their ruin on the Grand Canal, were indirectly subsidized by the spice-hungry English."

Elizabeth David
Spices, Salt and Aromatics in the English Kitchen

Until fairly recently the spice cabinet I have in my kitchen today would have made me a rich woman. For 5,000 years, through the end of the Renaissance, spices played the same role in the world economy that petroleum plays today. They came to Europe over difficult land routes or treacherous sea routes from India. If I'd lived in the thirteenth century I could have paid my rent, taxes and even my dowry in peppercorns; a pound of ginger would have bought me a sheep, two pounds of mace was worth a cow, and a pound of nutmeg was worth seven fat oxen. It was the spice trade that prompted the great sea explorations of the late fifteenth and sixteenth centuries. Were it not for the demand for these seasonings Vasco da Gama might have stayed at home, or at least continued to take the long route from Portugal to India. Christopher Columbus might never have discovered America, and Europe would not have known the pleasures of the spices, flavourings and foods indigenous to the New World (allspice, chilli peppers, vanilla, chocolate, potatoes and tomatoes, to name a few) until much later.

The word 'spice' has the same root as the word 'species,' meaning 'classes of object.' Spices are the aromatic parts—buds, bark, berries, fruit, seeds, roots or (in the case of saffron) flower stigmas—of certain plants, most of which are indigenous to hot or tropical countries. To westerners spices have always seemed exotic because they come, for the most part, from so far away.

The seeds of several herb plants, such as coriander, anise and fennel, are considered spices; this is where herbs and spices overlap. In this collection you will find some of these seeds (cumin, caraway and fennel, for example), which I also listed in my *Herbs and Honey Cookery*. I have seen these spices, as well as the capsicum peppers, listed in herbals, but they are considered by most to be spices. There seems to be a great deal of confusion as to the difference between herbs and spices. According to some, culinary herbs are one group of spices. I would define herbs as the leaves of annual and perennial plants which can be used fresh or dried to season dishes, as opposed to spices, which are usually, with the exception of ginger root, used in their dried state.

In any case, spices have been around for thousands of years. Ginger is mentioned in Chinese texts as far back as the fifth century B.C., and spices are well documented in ancient Hindu texts that date from Vedic times (third to first centuries B.C.). Egyptians imported cinnamon and cassia, essential elements in the embalming process, from the East during the Pyramid Age. In ancient times they were the basic ingredients of incense, embalming preservatives, ointments, cosmetics, perfumes, antidotes against poisons and medicines. The Greeks imported pepper, cassia, cinnamon, ginger, anise, caraway, poppy seeds, fennel, coriander, mint and garlic from the Far East through Alexandria, the most important trading centre between the Mediterranean and the Indian Ocean. Hippocrates mentions most of these in his medical treatises; over 400 of his preparations are still in use today.

It was not until the first century B.C. in Rome that spices began to be used to a greater extent in cooking. During the time of Pliny (who complains in his writings of the cost of pepper; he apparently didn't feel it was worth it) the use of spices as condiments and seasonings increased greatly, and consumption skyrocketed. Rome developed a very active spice trade with southern Arabia, Somaliland and India. There was a constant drain of gold to the East for these gastronomic treasures, which were indeed luxury items by the time they reached Rome. Once there, their prices had inflated by 100 times. This was due to shipwrecks, storms, robberies and perhaps most important, the greed of the Arab middlemen who imposed tremendous tariffs and tolls on the spice importers who were obliged to pass through Arabia on their journey back to Rome. The Arabs controlled the trade routes until the latter half of the first century A.D. They protected their interests by shrouding the origins of the spices in great mystery, maintaining that spices like cinnamon and cassia came from swampy African habitats guarded by huge, ferocious, winged, batlike creatures. Stories like these discouraged importers from attempting to make contact themselves with the real places of origin, China, India and Asia. But during the latter half of the first century A.D., the Greek merchant Hippalus figured out the seasonal nature of the monsoons in the Indian Ocean, which facilitated sea travel from Roman Egypt to India. From then on sailors knew that if they made the voyage from Egypt to India between April and October and the return trip between October and April, they could accomplish the round trip in one year instead of two. It was no longer advantageous to go overland. This broke the Arab monopoly, and spices came pouring into the Empire. The Romans became even more extravagant in their use of the condiments; the nobles even slept on saffron-filled pillows because this was believed to be an antidote to the terrible hangovers brought on by their sweet, heavily spiced wines.

Roman imperialism brought spices to the hands of the Goths, Vandals and Huns. Apparently the barbarians knew their value, for when the Gothic king Alaric made a deal with the Romans in 408 A.D. not to sack the city of Rome, along with his demands for gold, silver, silk tunics and valuable skins he demanded 3,000 pounds of peppercorns.

During the Dark Ages there was very little trading between Europe and the East because the Arabs had occupied Alexandria in 641, and the trade routes were no longer safe for European Christians. Mohammed himself had been an experienced spice merchant, having worked as a youth with a Meccan tradesman who dealt in spices with Syria and South Arabia. But the Crusades reopened trade with the East in the eleventh, twelfth and thirteenth centuries. This is when Venice, whose importance as a port and commercial centre was unparalleled, began to rise to the heights it would reach during the early Renaissance.

During the Middle Ages spices were used to mask the odours of decaying food and the putrefying fumes that hung over European towns. There was little variation in the diets of Medieval Europeans—no fruits or vegetables to speak of, mainly meat, fowl and hard, dry bread, and the meat, more often than not, was not fresh. Even today the demand for spices is highest in those countries where there is no refrigeration.

But during the Renaissance the standard of living in Europe improved, cooking and eating habits changed, and spices, which had been considered luxuries up until this time, became necessities. Perhaps the European imagination was captured by Marco Polo, who stimulated the Age of Exploration with his descriptions of Kublai Khan's court; his reports recounted numerous delectable, spicy repasts. Europeans became hungrier and hungrier for these exotic ingredients, and merchants and governments greedier. Spices played the major role in the commercial prosperity of this age.

By the middle of the fifteenth century, land routes to the East had become unsafe again due to the fall of Constantinople to the Turks. The Muslims were imposing extremely high tariffs on spices, and it became imperative for Europeans to open up new sea routes to the East if they wanted an economic future. The kings of Portugal and Spain encouraged sea exploration, and so began the Age of Exploration. It was at this time that Christopher Columbus, convinced he could reach India by sailing west, discovered America, and that Vasco da Gama sailed from Portugal around the Cape of Good Hope and on to India. The message he brought home from the king of India stated: '. . . My country is rich in cinnamon, cloves, ginger, pepper and precious stones. That which I ask in exchange is gold, silver, corals and scarlet cloth.' A fleet was fitted out immediately and was sent off. So ended the Venetian monopoly on spices, and thus began the European monopoly. Cinnamon, cloves and peppercorns would never again finance a doge's palace.

For the next 200 years the price of spices would serve as a barometer for the world economy, and the European demand would stimulate more exploration and colonization. Expeditions such as Magellan's circumnavigation of the globe from 1519 to 1522 and Cortes' conquest of Mexico in 1519, usually returned with only a handful of the men they had set out with, but always with the hulls of whatever ships remained packed with tons of cloves, nutmegs, mace and cinnamon as well as gold and silver.

It seems that almost all of the European countries profited from the spice trade (but not without inflicting savagely cruel, slavelike conditions on the natives of the countries they colonized). The English founded the East India Company in 1600. The Dutch, who grew rich by providing ships and crews and eventually began to expand their own trade to the Far East, founded the United Dutch East India Company in 1602 and eventually drove the Portuguese out of the Spice Islands. By the end of the seventeenth century, they controlled the spice trade, only to be defeated by the British a century later.

By the end of the eighteenth century, the United States had entered the market, especially in the West Indies, but also in Sumatra. From 1800 to 1811 Salem, Massachusetts, monopolized the Sumatra pepper trade, bringing in from 500 to as much as 1,200 tons a year.

But by the middle of the seventeenth century spices were no longer luxury items, as they were so much easier to obtain, nor were they necessary for masking the rancid flavours of foods, as now there was much more variety. In eighteenth century England the use of spices became a kind of fad, which Restoration playwrights did not hesitate to mock. We can still find pocket nutmeg graters and Georgian cinnamon casters dating from this time. People carried spices which they used to season the heavily spiced drinks which were then the rage.

Modern times have seen a decrease in the use of spices in the West, as food has become industrialized and synthetic spice essences and flavourings have begun to be manufactured. This is a pity, as nothing can really imitate their distinctive flavours. But recently, perhaps because of the influx of Asian and Latin American populations into Europe and North America, there has been a growing interest in exotic cuisines like Indian, Chinese, Mexican, Vietnamese, Thai and North African—the cuisines that make the most of spices. We in the West have always been comfortable with the sweet dessert spices like cinnamon, nutmeg and cloves, but on the whole we are not altogether at home with spices like cardamom, turmeric and cumin. But now that the world has become so small and spices of all kinds are quite easy to come by they needn't remain a mystery.

Cooking with Spices

The way to become comfortable with spices is to work with them, to become familiar with each one and learn the way they act upon the foods they are seasoning, as well as how they interact with each other. Each spice has unique and specific properties. Some are aromatics, some add heat to a dish, some lend colouring, others are souring agents and others act as thickeners. Some spices have more than one property; saffron, for example, is used to colour dishes, and at the same time it lends a marvellous, sweet aroma. Only a handful of spices are 'hot,' though when we use the word 'spicy,' hot is what we usually mean. Spices vary in fragrance, sweetness, aroma and heat. Sometimes a particular spice is intended to dominate a dish: at other times several are meant to blend together in a dish and not overwhelm. Despite the fact that 'spicy' has strong connotations to most people, some of the most successfully spiced dishes are very subtle. Spices are usually added to dishes in relatively small amounts.

Most spices must be cooked before they will release their fragrance. They release more of their aroma when slightly crushed.

In addition to culinary properties, spices, like herbs, have healing and medicinal properties. In Indian cuisine these properties have influenced their use in certain kinds of dishes. Asafoetida and ginger root counteract flatulence and colic, so they are often added to leguminous preparations. Fennel, cardamom and cloves stimulate the digestive system, curb nausea and provide relief from heartburn and indigestion, so they are chewed after Indian meals. Cloves act as an antiseptic and are often used in pickles. Fenugreek water is used as a tonic for gastritis and other stomach disorders; the soaked seeds are a very effective digestive aid and for this reason they are often added to Indian dahls and starchy vegetable dishes.

Spices also have an effect on body temperature. 'Warm spices' generate internal body heat and are recommended for cold weather. We find the warm spices—cardamom, cinnamon, powdered ginger, mace, nutmeg and hot red pepper—in the cuisines of the mountainous regions of Northern India. 'Cool spices' take away body heat. All the spices which are not 'warm' range from 'very cool' to 'moderately warm.' The after-dinner spices are all 'cool.'

One reason we find spicy dishes in hot, tropical countries is that in addition to the fact that these are the regions in which the spices grow, spices induce perspiration, which has a cooling effect. That's one reason why people in India drink hot tea laced with spices even in very hot weather.

The reason people sometimes have digestive problems after eating spiced food is that most spices are not easily digestible in their raw form. For this reason they should either be cooked in oil or simmered with food, or if added to an uncooked dish they should be dry-roasted first (although I often add very small amounts of uncooked spices like cumin, curry powder and chilli powder to uncooked foods like 'guacamole' and salad dressings).

When a recipe calls for several spices you should make sure to measure them out and have them ready by the stove before you begin to cook.

Buying, Storing and Grinding

Spices, like coffee, are infinitely more aromatic and complex if bought whole and freshly ground when you use them. Whole they will remain fresh for up to one year if properly stored in sealed jars in a cool, dry, dark place. Asafoetida, mustard seeds and fenugreek will stay fresh for up to three years.

Once spices are ground their aromatic oils begin to evaporate. It only takes minutes to grind your own. I keep an extra coffee mill for spices. Never use the mill you keep for coffee for spices. I learned this the first time I used my coffee mill to grind cinnamon sticks and cloves. From then on my coffee always tasted as if it were laced with spices because the blades and plastic cover retain some of the oils and resins of the spices (apparently these are more powerful than those in the coffee beans), and I was quickly obliged to buy myself another mill for coffee.

A recipe will often call for a small amount of a crushed spice or seeds. This is easily done in a mortar and pestle. Ceramic mortars like the Japanese suribachi and marble or brass mortars are the most efficient for this. You can also use a kitchen mallet or rolling pin. First place the spice in a plastic bag, and then pound on a flat surface.

For peppercorns my favourite mill is the sort you can adjust so that the pepper can be coarse or fine depending on the recipe. There are also handy mills on the market now that have a container on the bottom for quick measuring.

There are now some beautiful nutmeg graters available that are engineered like a peppermill, but with a small blade on the bottom that shaves the nutmeg and grates them down to the last flake. Standard nutmeg graters do the job too, of course, but with more damage to your fingers or knuckles when you get down to the end of the nutmeg. Look for the kind with a container for storing the nutmeg.

The French company SEB is now distributing its Minichop abroad. This has a detachable blade which makes for easy cleaning. But it doesn't powder as finely as a coffee mill, and like the electric coffee mill, the plastic container and blades will retain the resin and aroma of the spices, so don't plan on using your minichop for garlic and herbs as well as spices.

There are also attractive hand grinders on the market. They look like small grain mills which latch onto the edge of a table. They are handy for grinding large amounts of spices.

Food processors and blenders don't grind spices finely enough. My choice is the electric coffee mill, which is inexpensive and efficient.

Roasting Spices

Often recipes, especially for several Indian dishes, call for roasted, ground spices. These are roasted in a dry, heavy frying pan or griddle until they turn dark brown. To roast spices heat an Indian griddle ('kadhai') or a dry, heavy frying pan, preferably cast iron, for two minutes over medium heat. Add the spices and roast over medium heat, stirring constantly and shaking the pan so they don't burn. For the first minute or two nothing will happen, then suddenly the spices will begin to jump around, brown and smoke. Watch very carefully and stir constantly. Lower the heat a little if they seem to be browning too fast. When they are dark brown they are done. Transfer immediately to a cool, dry bowl and allow to cool. Grind, if instructed, to a fine powder in an electric or hand mill. The roasting time will depend on the size of the pan and the amount of spice as well as the kind of spice. On a standard Indian griddle 4 tablespoons of coriander seeds take 6 minutes, 4 tablespoons of cumin seeds take 8 minutes, and 1½ cups of garam masala takes 10 minutes.

Frying Spices

In many Indian recipes spices are fried in hot oil or fat to remove their raw taste and release their flavour into the oil before the other ingredients are added. The oil must be hot enough to allow the spices to brown quickly, but not so hot that they'll burn. Because I use less fat in my cooking than traditional Indian cooks, I fry the spices at a lower temperature for slightly longer to avoid burning. The results are the same; the perfume of the spices penetrates the other foods in the dish.

Whole spices should always be added to a dish before ground spices, and the heat should be a little lower for ground spices. Mustard seeds and fenugreek cook more slowly than other spices in their whole state. When mustard seeds are fried they pop like popcorn, which releases their flavour. Unpopped they are chewy and bitter. When frying mustard seeds in oil have a lid handy to protect yourself from spluttering seeds and oil.

Freezing Spiced Food

When food is frozen the ice crystals rupture cell walls and flavour constituents are released. For this reason spicy foods will be spicier if frozen and thawed. This is something to consider when you are making piquant foods for the freezer. Be cautious with your peppery ingredients. You can always add more after you've tested the thawed dish.

A Glossary of Spices

Some of the spices I have listed here also appear in my *Herb and Honey Cookery* (Thorsons, 1984). As I explained earlier in this section, this is because there seems to be some confusion as to whether the seeds of certain herb plants, like cumin and caraway, fall under the category of herbs or spices, and I have seen these, as well as the capsicum peppers, listed in herbals. But having read numerous definitions of spices since beginning this book, I now concede that those ingredients which I also listed in my herb book are indeed spices.

Allspice   Whole allspice (or pimento) berries are the fruits of the *Pimenta dioica* tree, native to the West Indies and Latin America. The round berries, slightly larger than peppercorns, are picked green and are dried in the sun, whereupon they take on their rusty-brown colour. Like all spices, it is best to purchase allspice berries whole and grind them as you use them.

Outside the U.S. allspice is known as **pimento** because the Spaniards, thinking the berries resembled peppercorns in flavour, named the spice **pimiento** when they discovered it in the West Indies. It is the only major spice grown on a commercial basis exclusively in the Western Hemisphere. Most of it (and the best) is grown in Jamaica, although it is also grown in Guatemala, Brazil, Mexico, Honduras and the Leeward Islands.

The name allspice derives from the flavour of this sweet, fragrant spice, which is reminiscent of several of the sweet spices, most notably cinnamon and cloves, with a hint of nutmeg and pepper.

The spice is used all over the world to sweeten and spice baked goods, as a pickling spice and in many Middle Eastern dishes. It can surprise the palate in the most pleasing way when it occurs in a Moroccan carrot, beet or orange salad.

Anise seeds   Anise seeds are native to Asia Minor, the Greek Islands and Egypt and were used by the ancient Egyptians, Greeks and Romans to sweeten and flavour food and beverages. They have a sweet, liquorice flavour and are used as a flavouring for sweets, breads and other baked goods. They are also the flavouring agent for the various liquorice-flavoured liqueurs and cordials popular all over the Mediterranean. Pastis, Anisette, Ouzo and Arak are all flavoured with anise, as well as with fennel and star anise. The ground seeds are also often an ingredient in Indian curries, particularly vegetarian and fish dishes from Bengal. The seeds, slightly roasted, are chewed after Indian meals to aid digestion.

Star Anise   Star anise, a native of China and important in Chinese cuisine, is the star-shaped fruit of an evergreen tree belonging to the magnolia family. The spice has a liquorice flavour that is stronger and slightly more bitter than that of anise. It is an ingredient in Chinese Five Spice and can be found in Oriental markets.

Asafoetida (or *Asafetida*)   This is a strange ingredient which is used in very small amounts in Indian cooking. It is a combination of various dried gum resins of Indian and Iranian plants and can be bought in lump and powdered form in Indian markets. Buy the lump form if possible because asafoetida does not release its rather unpleasant odour (not unlike bad garlic or onions) unless it is powdered.

A lump of asafoetida about the size of a pea will undergo a mysterious change when heated in oil; the aroma and flavour mellow and resemble mild onions. It is used in the cuisine of the strictest Hindu sects, who believe that onions and garlic are too strong. They feel that the two should never be used together.

Capsicum peppers   This is the family of peppers indigenous to the New World that includes cayenne, the hot peppers used in Asian cuisine and those used in Mexican cooking and the different grades of Hungarian paprika. It is a very diverse family because the peppers breed prodigiously and crossbreed easily (there are over 200 capsicum peppers in existence, of which 100 can be found in Mexico alone); so it can be very confusing, especially since some of the names change when the peppers are used in their dried state.

The heat of the various capsicum peppers varies from one to the other. It seems that the smaller peppers are the most fiery. Some of those used in Indonesian and Asian cuisines outstrip the Mexican peppers by a longshot; I'm always flabbergasted by how much heat can be contained in one speck of a little pepper. There is also great variation in our tolerance for hot peppers. This seems to be genetic; some people can gobble down whole jalapenos without blinking an eye, whereas others take one bite and are in agony—their noses run, their eyes water and their palate is finished for the evening. Research has recently shown that hot peppers trigger the release of endorphins, which may explain why some people seem to get so high from them. As for antidotes for the heat, water is of no use whatsoever. I've had the best luck eating a piece of bread, which seems to absorb some of the heat.

The following are those most commonly used in Mexican, European and Asian cuisines (there are many more peppers that you would come across in markets in Mexico and Asian countries, but these are the ones you can find outside these countries).

Paprika   Also known as Hungarian pepper and Spanish pepper, this is the national spice of Hungary. Paprika is the dried powder of a mild, sweet, bright red pepper. It is extremely high in vitamin C and carotene, and it stimulates circulation. It should have a mild, sweet flavour, and you should use it in large quantities, a teaspoon or more at a time. It must be very fresh (if the colour has gone from bright red to rust brown, it has deteriorated) or it will be bitter. Store it in the refrigerator in an airtight container. There are eight grades of Hungarian paprika, ranging from mild and sweet to hot and very rich. Always look for the word 'Hungarian' or 'Magyar' on the package, or even better,

'Kalocsa' or 'Szeged,' two cities in the heart of the paprika region. **Indian paprika** has a pungent aroma and a sweet taste and is used in many Kashmiri preparations. I use paprika most often in soups, bean dishes and vegetable dishes.

Chile Serrano   These are small, narrow, dark green chillies (sometimes they ripen to red) about 1½ inches (3cm) long on the average and a little less than ½ inch (1cm) wide. They are used in many Mexican recipes (see the Salsas on page 173, for instance) and are very hot, with a fresh, vibrant flavour. They will keep for several weeks if kept dry and stored at the bottom of the refrigerator. Separate out any that are soft or turning and wrap the rest in a paper towel. Do not keep in a plastic bag, as they will release moisture and will rot sooner. The peppers may wrinkle, but they will still be good.

Chillies serranos can also be frozen. First toast them in a dry frying pan or on a griddle until the skin blisters and turns brown and they are soft, or boil them in water for 10 minutes and then drain. Freeze in plastic bags, and use as needed.

Ripened, dried serranos are sold as *serranos secos* or *chile japones*. They are also sold canned in a pickling medium called *escabeche*.

Serranos can be used in all recipes calling for small, hot, green chillies.

Chile Jalapeño   This is the other small, green chilli most often used in its fresh or pickled state in Mexican dishes. Jalapeños are mid- to dark-green with a smooth surface and a more rounded tip than the serrano. They are about 2½ inches (5cm) long on the average and about ¾ inch (1½ cm) wide at the widest part, a fatter chilli than the serrano. They are quite hot, but not quite as vibrantly 'picante' as the serrano. I use them interchangeably for salsas and other Mexican preparations.

Jalapeños can be stored in the same way as serranos. They are fairly easy to find canned in *escabeche* and are widely used in this form as a condiment with Mexican food. They are also quite good stuffed (see recipe, page 185). Fresh or canned, jalapeños are a necessary garnish for *nachos* (see page 183).

When jalapeños are ripened and smoked they become *chiles chipotles*. These can be found canned in escabeche or in a red *adobo* sauce (they are the most popular in this pickled state), or dried, in stores that sell Mexican ingredients. They have a distinctive piquant, smoky flavour.

Jalapeños can be used in all recipes calling for hot, green chilli peppers.

Cayenne   In Mexico and India this pepper is used fresh, it is mid-green and is about 3 inches (6cm) long and ¾ inch (2cm) wide. For the most part, though, it is ripened to red and is usually used in its dried state, either whole, crushed or ground. It is extremely hot—a little goes a long way. Just a few grains will add heat to any dish. You will find it in most of the spicy Indian recipes, and it is a must in Cajun cuisine.

Chile Poblano   These are large, undulating, triangular-shaped peppers with a dark green (sometimes almost black), shiny skin. Their size averages about 3 inches (6cm) wide at the top and 5 inches (10cm) long, tapering down to a point. Although poblanos can be quite 'picante', on the average they are relatively mild, and their flavour is very rich and aromatic. They are usually roasted and peeled before using (this enhances their flavour even more), and are used for the stuffed chillies ('chiles rellenos') we find in Mexican and Southwestern cuisines. Roasted and cut into strips, they become 'rajas,' which are used in many vegetable dishes and casseroles. Once roasted and peeled they can be frozen in plastic bags and used as needed.

When dried the chile poblano becomes the *chile ancho*. These have a deep reddish-brown colour and a wrinkled skin. The basis for many of the red chilli sauces in Mexican and Southwestern cooking (see 'Mole Sauce,' page 187), they are probably the most widely used chilli in Mexico.

Anaheim Chilli   These are also known as the California Chilli, the Chile Verde, the Long, Green Chilli and Big Jim (all different chillies but close enough to be interchanged in recipes). They are long, narrow and slightly twisted, with colours ranging from light to dark green, and sometimes ripened to yellow, orange and red. The flavour is peppery and fresh, ranging from mild to hot. They are found in most American markets, and are good stuffed or minced to add spice to various dishes.

Chile Pasilla   This is the dried form of the *chile chilaca*, a long, slim, very dark green chilli averaging 6 inches (12cm) in length and 1 inch (2cm) wide. It is very hot and has a rich, dusky flavour. It is used in combination with the Chile Ancho in sauces like Mole (page 187). Because of its dark, almost black colour the chili pasilla is sometimes referred to as the *chile negro*.

Pepperoncini   This is the hot pepper used in Italian cuisine and pickled and sold as the Italian pickled pepper. The peppers are small, twisted and have a pale green colour.

Chile Mulato   Another dried Mexican chilli roughly the same shape as the *ancho* but with a tougher, slightly less wrinkled skin. It is brownish black and often difficult to distinguish from the *ancho*. The flavour is a bit sweeter than that of the *ancho*.

Chile Guajillo   A long, pointed, slender, dried Mexican chilli averaging 4½ inches (9cm) long and 1¼ inches (2½cm) wide. It is extremely 'picante.'

Chile Cascabel   A small, round, dried Mexican chilli with a brownish-red, smooth skin. It sounds like a rattle when you shake it. It is less 'picante' than the guajillo and has a nice, nutty flavour when toasted and ground for sauces.

Chile Seco   Another dried chilli from the Yucatan and Campeche regions of Mexico. These taste a little like hot paprika, which can be substituted for the peppers. They are small and bright red in colour.

Chinese Hot Peppers   These are used in hot Szechuan and Hunan dishes and can be pretty fiery. Sometimes you can find them in flake form in Chinese groceries, sometimes ground. In authentic regional Chinese cooking specific peppers from each region are used, but these are not always easy to find. If you can't find Chinese peppers, substitute cayenne. Mexican peppers would be too sweet.

Chinese Hot Pepper Oil   Oil seasoned with Chinese hot peppers. Extremely hot. Found in Chinese groceries.

Storing Dried Peppers   Dried peppers will keep indefinitely if they have been dried under good conditions and are stored in a cool, dry place. Check every few months and remove any that may be deteriorating. I store mine in large, tightly sealed jars in the pantry.

Caraway seeds   These seeds have a distinctive flavour I always associate with Jewish rye bread. People either like the flavour or hate it, so it's best not to serve dishes heavily seasoned with the seeds to people whose tastes are not familar to you. They are a common ingredient in German and Austrian cuisines. I love the seeds in breads, potato soups and grain soups, and some salads.

Cardamom seeds   These are small, black, fragrant seeds which come in black, green or white pods (white pods are actually green pods which have been bleached). Black cardamom, which is more fragrant than green cardamom, is only available in speciality stores and Indian markets. Green cardamom can always be substituted for black. Cardamom has a distinctive earthy-perfume flavour and aroma. One of the key ingredients in Mughal garam masala, it is commonly used in Indian dishes as well as in spice breads and cakes. The whole pods are often added to pilafs and vegetable dishes; they give off their marvellous aroma as the dishes cook. They are not meant to be eaten in this whole state, but no harm will be done if they are.

Carom   Carom is the seed of the lovage plant and is used in Indian dishes. The seeds look like celery seeds and have a sharp, hot taste and thyme-like aroma. It is sold in Indian grocery stores and is used as a flavouring in Indian vegetable dishes, breads and savoury pastries.

Chinese Five Spice   This is a Chinese mixture of equal parts ground anise pepper (a close relative of anise with a more pungent flavour), star anise, cassia (a close relative of cinnamon, also with a more pungent flavour), cloves and fennel seed. The mixture has a sweet, subtle flavour and is an ingredient in many Oriental dishes. It can be found in Chinese and Vietnamese groceries or you can make it yourself.

Cinnamon and *Cassia*   These are both sold interchangeably as cinnamon although they are derived from different trees. They have almost identical sweet, pungent flavours, cassia being slightly more pungent, and are used in the West to flavour sweets and baked foods, syrups, hot mulled ciders, wines and punches. In Indian cooking cinnamon is an important ingredient in pilafs and is one of the ingredients in Mughal garam masala (page 25). I use it to heighten the flavours of an Italian tomato sauce: a tiny pinch of cinnamon added just at the end brings out the sweetness of the tomatoes and the aroma of the garlic and other herbs. It's a trick that surprises many people, but it always works.

Cinnamon and cassia are the barks of the cinnamon and cassia trees. The spices are at their best when freshly ground, but for baking it is sometimes difficult to get a fine enough grind, so using powdered cinnamon is preferable. Have both sticks and ground cinnamon on hand, but don't let the powdered cinnamon get too old. Whole sticks of cinnamon are used to flavour Indian pilafs and are removed after cooking.

Cassia is one of the oldest of all spices. It is recorded in China in 2500 B.C. and in Egypt in 1600 B.C. It came into Europe over the spice routes.

Cloves   Cloves are the dried buds of an evergreen tree native to the Molucca Islands in eastern Indonesia. They have a sweet, strong, pungent flavour and aroma. A little goes a long way. It's best to buy cloves whole and grind them as you need them. In Indian cooking they are used in pilafs and other preparations in their whole and powdered form, and they are an ingredient in Mughal garam masala. They have antiseptic properties, which is one reason why they are an ingredient in pickling. They are commonly used in spiced and mulled wines, ciders and punches, spice breads and cakes.

Coriander Seeds These light brown spherical seeds, slightly larger than peppercorns, have a completely different flavour than the fresh leaves of the plant (the leaves are an herb, the seeds a spice). The flavour is mild and sort of musky-sweet, with a subtle hint of orange peel. They are widely used in Indian cooking, both whole and ground, and are an essential ingredients in garam masala (page 26). In Indian cuisine they are often roasted before being ground (see section on roasting spices, page 14). In their raw, powdered form they can serve as a thickener in Indian sauces and gravies.

In France coriander seeds are an essential ingredient in vegetables cooked 'a la Grecque,' and they are called for in 'Pain d'Epices' (page 50). In English and North American cooking it is an important pickling spice and is found in spice breads and cakes. It also occurs in several Middle Eastern and North African dishes.

Cumin Seeds Cumin seeds in their whole and ground states are an essential ingredient in Mexican, Indian and North African cuisines. The spice has a very special, unmistakable nutty-earthy aroma. The seeds are light brown in colour and resemble caraway seeds in appearance, but their flavour is totally different. Ground, roasted cumin is added to many Indian raitas and appetizers and should be kept on hand (see instructions for roasting and grinding, page 14). I add cumin to several cheese and vegetables dishes (it is especially good with potatoes), and sometimes to breads.

Curry Powder Curry powder is not one spice but is a blend of several spices. The name derives from the Indian word 'kari,' which can mean either the sweet aromatic leaves of the kari plant, used in southern and southwestern Indian regional cooking, or a south Indian technique of preparing stir-fried vegetables, which involves a spice blend called 'kari podi' (curry powder). The classic kari podi blend includes roasted, ground turmeric, red pepper, coriander, black pepper, cumin, fenugreek, kari leaves, mustard seeds and sometimes cinnamon and cloves. The earliest British merchants who colonised India probably took this powder back to England with them so they could mimic the flavours and aromas they had grown fond of in India. Without much knowledge or understanding of authentic Indian cuisine they would add this powder to meat and vegetable dishes, which eventually became known as 'curries.' As English influence spread into the north and east of India, new ingredients found their way into curry powder, while at the same time the word 'curry' became very popular within the English-speaking Indian middle class. Eventually simple Indian dishes with spiced gravies, known as 'salans,' became known as curries even though these dishes bear no resemblance to the dishes we in the West know as 'curries.'

In true Indian cuisine the balance of fresh spices is so important that curry powder would never work, especially since curry powders vary in heat and pungency and often contain ingredients never used in certain regional dishes. Indians do use premixed blends—garam masala and Mughal garam masala—but these are used only as a base for spicing a dish (see pages 25–26).

The European curry powders can, however, lend a very pleasant flavour to a dish, and I use this seasoning frequently. Care must be taken, though, when purchasing curry powders, as some are much hotter and fresher than others. Bad curry powders taste bitter, like little more than turmeric. This is one spice worth looking for in the best imported spice shops.

The ingredients most often used in curry powders are the following: black pepper, dried red chillies, cloves, cinnamon, cardamom, coriander seeds, cumin seeds, curry leaves, fenugreek seeds, dried ginger (sometimes), mace or nutmeg (sometimes), mustard seeds and turmeric.

Fennel Seeds   These seeds of the fennel herb plant have a liquorice flavour like anise and can be used interchangeably. They are not quite as strong as anise. Fennel has been cultivated in India since Vedic times and is also native to southern Europe; it was popular among the Romans, who spread it to other parts of the continent.

Fenugreek seeds   The seeds of fenugreek, an annual herb which is a member of the bean family, are native to Asia Minor and India. Fenugreek is an important ingredient in Indian cooking. The small, hard, vaguely triangular seeds have a very strong aroma and bitter taste. Recipes call for a very few, and they impart a distinctive curry flavour. They are known to be a digestive, and for this reason are often cooked with legumes.

Ginger   In its fresh state ginger root is one of my favourite spices. It is pungent and aromatic without being overwhelmingly piquant, and finds its place in all kinds of dishes, dishes that range from soups to vegetable, grain and tofu dishes to salads and desserts. Entire cook books have been devoted to this spice. A common ingredient in Indian, Chinese and Japanese cuisines, it is easy to find in Oriental markets and some supermarkets. Look for smooth, unshriveled roots. To prepare fresh ginger, peel and thinly slice, then chop very fine or cut in shreds, depending on the recipe. Fresh, peeled ginger can also be grated or minced in a food processor. To store the roots, place in a jar of sherry in the refrigerator. It will keep indefinitely.

Dried ginger, usually found in its powdered form, has a much different flavour than fresh and is used in different kinds of dishes. In Indian cuisine it is used in Moghul dishes to lend a piquant or sour taste and sweet, woody fragrance. I find the spice rather bitter and try not to substitute it for fresh ginger when that is what a recipe calls for. But dried ginger is a particularly welcome ingredient in many spiced breads and cakes, especially Pain d'Epices (page 50), Gingerbread (page 223) and Gingersnaps (page 234).

Mace   Mace and nutmeg are both part of the fruit of the nutmeg tree and are native to the Molucca Islands. Mace is the lining of the nutmeg; it is carefully peeled off the shell and dried until it becomes brittle and yellowish brown in colour. The dried membranes are sold commercially as mace blades or are ground as mace (as usual, the blades are preferable). Its flavour is similar to nutmeg, but stronger, and the two should not be used interchangeably. Mace is an ingredient in several Indian and Kashmiri dishes and is a spice in several European and American cakes and sweets.

Mango Powder   This is derived from dried, unripened mangos which are ground to a buff-coloured powder. The powder has a pungent aroma and is used to impart a sour taste to certain Indian dishes.

Mustard Seeds   Two kinds of mustard seeds are commonly used. *Black mustard seeds* (also called Brown Mustard and Indian Mustard) look a bit like poppy seeds but are larger. They are indispensable in southern and southwestern Indian cuisines, and they are used as a pickling spice and flavouring for vegetable dishes in North Indian cuisine. The seeds have a pungent aroma and a slightly bitter, slightly sour flavour. They are usually sautéed in hot oil just until they stop spluttering, then are stirred into a dish (such as a dahl) to impart a distinct yet subtle tang. They are available in Indian markets.

Yellow or *white mustard seeds* are the seeds ground to make dry mustard powder and all prepared mustards. The pungency of prepared mustards is due to an oil which is released when the seeds are ground or crushed and mixed with water. An enzyme causes the bitter substance in the mustard, glucoside, to react with the water, and the hot flavour emerges. Powdered mustard, therefore, once mixed with cold water, must be allowed to stand for 10 minutes so that the hot flavour can emerge. Boiling water will kill the enzyme and the resulting mustard will be mild and bitter tasting. Mustard seeds act as a preservative, one reason they are widely used in pickling. They have been used as a spice for thousands of years.

Nutmeg   The inner part of the fruit of the nutmeg tree, this spice has a delicious sweet, nutty flavour. It is commonly used in Moghul and Kashmiri cooking and is one of the ingredients in Mughal garam masala (see page 25). In western cuisines it is one of the sweet spices in baked goods and sweets, but it is also used to season soups, vegetables (especially spinach), cream sauces and many pasta and cheese dishes. It should always be freshly grated as it will quickly lose its zesty aroma in its powdered form. Nutmeg is one of my favourite spices. It gives many of my vegetable fillings for crêpes and pasta a mysterious and wonderful lift, and I often season fruit pastries and desserts with it. It goes especially well with bananas. The spice should be used with discretion, as the flavour can overpower a dish. It is especially useful for those on a salt-free diet.

Peppercorns (black and white)   Peppercorns, noted over 3,000 years ago in Sanskrit texts for their medicinal and preservative effects, are native to India and found their way from there to China and Europe. They are by far the most important spice in world trade today, claiming 25 percent of the market; 160 million pounds of peppercorns are sold annually. Although you see black pepper everywhere, you may not be aware of the subtle differences between the different kinds of peppercorns, and the different effects various grinds will have on the palate. Fine-quality black peppercorns smell and taste richly aromatic and full bodied; poor-quality peppercorns smell musty and one dimensional. Canned and ground peppercorns are stale and should not even be considered; they have a sharp, metallic taste, and they don't resemble freshly ground pepper at all.

It's amazing how such a commonly used spice can change the face of a dish. A few coarse grinds into a green salad will add an entire dimension, as it will to soups and vegetable dishes. In quantity, ground pepper will add fire to a dish. This is the hot ingredient in Chinese Hot and Sour Soup.

There are several varieties of black peppercorns. They are all berries that are picked green and are allowed to ferment for several days, then are dried in the sun until shriveled and blackish brown. The core of the berry remains white. *Tellicherry*, from the northern Malabar coast, has a rich aroma and big taste, spicy but not sharp. *Brazilian*, harvested along the Amazon River, is much like the Tellicherry, with an herbal scent and subtle hotness. *Malabar*, from the southern Malabar coast, is very aromatic and hot, with a slightly minty aftertaste. *Lampong*, from southern Sumatra, is tannic and sharp, with relatively little aroma.

White peppercorns are berries picked when they are fully mature and soaked in water for eight days until soft, then hulled. The grey inner cores are washed and sun dried until bleached white. They are hotter than black peppercorns and are less aromatic.

Mignonette Pepper is a mix of white and black peppercorns, which brings together the aroma of black and the strength of white pepper. The ratio of black to white is usually four parts black to one part white.

Green Peppercorns are picked immature and are marketed in their undried, soft state. They are best bought fresh or freeze dried, or bottled in natural juices (not brine) with no preservatives. They are often mashed to a paste and added to sauces and butters.

Red Peppercorns, usually sold freeze dried or bottled in natural juices, have a marvellous distinctive flavour which is more herbal than spicy. I flavour stuffings, grains and salads with them.

Pickling Spice   The proportions of the different spices vary in pickling spices, but they usually consist of black peppercorns, red chillies, mustard seeds, allspice, cloves, ginger (sometimes), mace and coriander seeds.

Poppy Seeds   Most common in or on breads and pastries, these tiny grey-black seeds have a pleasant, nutty flavour when baked. Ground white poppy seeds are used in Indian cooking to thicken gravies. When they are roasted before being ground the seeds impart a pleasant, nutty aroma similar to Chinese sesame oil to their dishes.

Saffron   This is the most luxurious and expensive of spices. It is the dried stigmas of the flowers of the saffron plant, a member of the crocus family. It is so costly (it retails at $2,000 a pound!) because it takes about 250,000 dried stigmas, collected from about 75,000 flowers, to make a pound of saffron. It is usually sold by the twentieth of an ounce or by the gram in thread and powdered form. I buy the threads, as powdered saffron is often adulterated. In Paris I buy my saffron at the pharmacy, where it is used in some homeopathic preparations.

Saffron's magic lies in the gorgeous yellow hue it imparts to its dishes and its strong, sweet, vaguely sealike aroma. I have sometimes had a hard time convincing strict vegetarians that there is no seafood in my vegetarian paella.

A little of this spice goes a long way, luckily. It only takes ¼ teaspoon to colour and flavour a cup of rice. To achieve even colouring and flavouring, powder the saffron threads with your fingers or the back of a spoon in a small bowl and soak in a little hot water or milk for 15 minutes. Add this solution, with the threads, to whatever you are cooking.

Tamarind   Although this isn't a spice, but the pulpy pod of a tropical plant, I'm including it in this list because it is often used to impart a sour flavour to Indian dishes. The pulp of the mature tamarind pods is compressed into balls or cakes, which are sold in Indian and Asian grocery stores. It tastes like very sour prunes. The flavour is extracted by soaking the tamarind in boiling water, then mashing the pulp and straining. This juice is used as a souring agent.

Turmeric   Turmeric is native to India and belongs to the ginger family. The roots are cleaned, boiled, dried and ground to a deep ochre-coloured powder. It is one of the main ingredients in curry powder. Turmeric imparts a lovely yellow colour to dishes and has a woody and, in my opinion, slightly bitter flavour. It is an important sacred spice in Hindu religions.

Vanilla   Not a spice but an aromatic, vanilla lends fragrance to syrups, pastries and sweet dessert sauces. It is the pod of a climbing orchid native to the rain forests of the New World. The Aztecs used it as a flavouring for chocolate. We use it to flavour sweet dishes.

Vanilla beans are picked unripe and are cured. They are dark brown with a shiny, flexible, tough skin. To extract their flavour for syrups and sauces, cut them in half lengthwise and simmer the beans, then remove them. Use pure vanilla extract in baked goods.

Spice Blends

In Indian cooking spice blends are called 'masalas,' which means a blend of several aromatic spices. In Indian homes masalas are sometimes pastes and are made by grinding herbs and seasonings along with the spices. The masalas are what give regional Indian dishes their distinctive flavours. Authentic garam masalas must be made at home. The following Mughal garam masala and garam masala are Julie Sahni's blend, from her *Classic Indian Cooking* (William Morrow and Co., 1980).

Mughal Garam Masala

(12 tablespoons, or ¾ cup)

This is essential to most North Indian preparations. It is usually added to a dish at the end, just before serving, to enhance the flavours of other ingredients. In some recipes, however, it is added at the beginning. This blend is subtle and mellow, with a cardamom flavour. In India it is used in cream-, milk-, yogurt- and fruit-sauce based dishes.

Imperial (Metric)	American
½ cup (about 60) black, or ⅓ cup (about 20) green or white cardamom pods	½ cup (about 60) black, or ⅓ cup (about 20) green or white cardamom pods
2 cinnamon sticks, 3 inches (6 cm) long	2 cinnamon sticks, 3 inches (6 cm) long
1 tablespoon whole cloves	1 tablespoon whole cloves
1 tablespoon black peppercorns	1 tablespoon black peppercorns
1½ teaspoons grated nutmeg (optional)	1½ teaspoons grated nutmeg (optional)

Remove the seeds from the cardamom pods. Crush the cinnamon stick with a kitchen mallet or rolling pin and combine with the other spices, except the nutmeg, and grind to a fine powder. Mix in the grated nutmeg, if desired. Store in an airtight container in a cool place.

Garam Masala

(12 tablespoons, or ¾ cup)

This is a more pungent, spicy version of the masala, containing large quantities of coriander and cumin. It is used in North Indian cooking. If you wish to make this hotter, increase the amount of peppercorns.

Imperial (Metric)	American
1½ tablespoons (about 10) black or 1 tablespoon green cardamom pods	1½ tablespoons (about 10) black or 1 tablespoon green cardamom pods
3 cinnamon sticks, 3 inches (6 cm) long	3 cinnamon sticks, 3 inches (6 cm) long
1½ teaspoons whole cloves	1½ teaspoons whole cloves
2 tablespoons black peppercorns	2 tablespoons black peppercorns
4 tablespoons cumin seeds	4 tablespoons cumin seeds
4 tablespoons coriander seeds	4 tablespoons coriander seeds

Remove the seeds from the cardamom pods. Crush the cinnamon with a kitchen mallet or rolling pin and combine with the other spices. Roast them in a dry frying pan or griddle (see roasting instructions, page 14), and grind to a fine powder. Store in an airtight container in a cool place.

Elizabeth David's Spice Blend

This is a sweet, peppery spice blend which makes a marvellous addition to breads.

Imperial (Metric)	American
1 large nutmeg, grated	1 large nutmeg, grated
1 6-inch (12cm) stick cinnamon	1 6-inch stick cinnamon
1 tablespoon white peppercorns or allspice berries	1 tablespoon white peppercorns or allspice berries
2 scant teaspoons, or about 30, cloves	2 scant teaspoons, or about 30, cloves
1½ teaspoons dried ginger, or a piece about 2-inches (5cm) long	1½ teaspoons dried ginger, or a piece about 2-inches long

Break up the cinnamon stick and grate the nutmeg. Place them, along with the other ingredients, in a spice mill and grind to a powder. Keep in a covered jar in a cool, dark place.

1. Breads

Buckwheat-Sesame Crackers with Fennel

(3 to 4 dozen)

Imperial (Metric)	American
4 teaspoons fennel seeds	4 teaspoons fennel seeds
6 oz (170g) wholemeal flour	1½ cups whole wheat flour
1 oz (30g) buckwheat flour	¼ cup buckwheat flour
1 oz (30g) sesame seeds	¼ cup sesame seeds
½ teaspoon sea salt	½ teaspoon sea salt
2 fl oz (60ml) safflower or vegetable oil	¼ cup safflower or vegetable oil
3 fl oz (90ml) water	⅓ cup water

1 Preheat the oven to 350 degrees F (180°C, gas mark 4). Oil 2 cookie sheets.

2 Place the fennel seeds in a mortar and pestle and crack.

3 Mix together the flours, sesame seeds, salt and cracked fennel seeds. Add the oil and cut in by taking the flour up by handfuls and rolling briskly between the palms of your hands. (This can also be done in a food processor.)

4 Add the water. The dough should have a pie crust consistency (though coarser). If too dry, add a little more water. Gather up the dough and roll out on a well-floured board or between pieces of greaseproof (waxed) paper. Dough should be about ⅛ inch thick.

5 Cut into squares or use a biscuit (cookie) cutter. Place on the prepared baking sheets and bake in the preheated oven until brown, about 20 to 25 minutes, switching the positions of the baking sheets halfway through the baking. Don't let them get too brown or they'll taste bitter. Cool on racks.

Yeasted Spice Bread with Courgettes (Zucchini) and Raisins

(2 loaves)

Imperial (Metric)	American
1 tablespoon active dry yeast	1 tablespoon active dry yeast
4 fl oz (120ml) lukewarm water	½ cup lukewarm water
4 fl oz (120 ml) lukewarm milk	½ cup lukewarm milk
2 fl oz (60 ml) mild-flavoured honey	¼ cup mild-flavored honey
1 egg	1 egg
2 tablespoons melted butter	2 tablespoons melted butter
1 tablespoon Elizabeth David's Spice Mix (page 27)	1 tablespoon Elizabeth David's Spice Mix (page 27)
1½ teaspoons salt	1½ teaspoons salt
2 teaspoons grated orange rind	2 teaspoons grated orange rind
½ lb (225g) shredded courgettes	1½ cups shredded zucchini
1 oz (30g) bran	¼ cup bran
¾ lb (340g) wholemeal flour	3 cups whole wheat flour
5 oz (140g) stoneground maize	1 cup stone-ground cornmeal
4 oz (115g) unbleached white flour, plus up to 4 oz (115g) additional for kneading	1 cup unbleached white flour plus up to 1 more cup additional for kneading
6 oz (170g) raisins	1 cup raisins
1 beaten egg, if desired, for brushing the loaves	1 beaten egg, if desired, for brushing the loaves

_1_ Dissolve the yeast in the water. Add the milk and honey, and beat in the egg and butter. Stir in the spice mix, salt, grated orange rind and the courgettes (zucchini). Fold in the bran and the maize (corn meal). Begin adding the flour (not including the additional unbleached white flour for kneading), a cup at a time, and fold in after each addition. When all the flour has been added, let the dough rest in the bowl for 15 minutes.

2 Turn out the dough on a well-floured work surface and knead for 10 minutes, or until the dough is smooth. Add flour as necessary. The dough is very moist, and it might be easier to knead by picking up the dough and throwing it against your floured work surface, rather than folding and leaning into the dough. Just take up the dough, slap it down on the table, take it up again, etc. This is also an effective way to develop the gluten.

3 Rinse, dry and oil your bowl. Place the dough in it rounded side down first, then rounded side up. Cover and let rise in a warm place for 45 minutes to an hour, or until doubled in bulk.

4 Punch down the dough, turn out onto a floured surface and knead in the raisins. Divide the dough in half and form into rounds or small loaves. Let rise on a greased baking sheet or in greased bread pans for 45 minutes to an hour, or until doubled.

5 Preheat the oven to 375 degrees F (190°C, gas mark 5). Slash the loaves and brush with water or egg. Bake 35 to 45 minutes, or until they sound hollow when tapped. Remove from the pans and cool on a rack.

Hot Cross Buns

(2 dozen)

Imperial (Metric)	American
8 fl oz (225ml) milk	1 cup milk
1 tablespoon active dry yeast	1 tablespoon active dry yeast
2 fl oz (60ml) mild-flavoured honey	¼ cup mild-flavored honey
4 tablespoons unsalted butter, melted and cooled	4 tablespoons unsalted butter, melted and cooled
2 eggs	2 eggs
¾ lb (340g) wholemeal pastry flour	3 cups whole wheat pastry flour
1 teaspoon sea salt	1 teaspoon sea salt
2 teaspoons Elizabeth David's Spice Blend* (see below)	2 teaspoons Elizabeth David's Spice Blend* (see below)
4 oz (115g) currants	⅔ cup currants
4 oz (115g) unbleached white flour, as needed	1 cup unbleached white flour, as needed
1 egg white	1 egg white

For the Glaze	For the Glaze
2 tablespoons lemon juice	2 tablespoons lemon juice
1 tablespoon mild-flavoured honey	1 tablespoon mild-flavored honey

*Elizabeth David's Spice Blend	*Elizabeth David's Spice Blend
1 large nutmeg, grated	1 large nutmeg, grated
¼ oz (7g), or 1 tablespoon white or black peppercorns *or* allspice berries	1 tablespoon white or black peppercorns *or* allspice berries
1 6-inch (12cm) cinnamon stick	1 6-inch cinnamon stick
2 teaspoons (or about 30) cloves	2 teaspoons (or about 30) cloves
⅛ oz (3½g), or 1½ teaspoons powdered ginger or dried ginger root	1½ teaspoons powdered ginger (⅛ ounce dried ginger root)

Combine all the ingredients and grind to a powder in a spice mill. Store in a well-sealed jar.

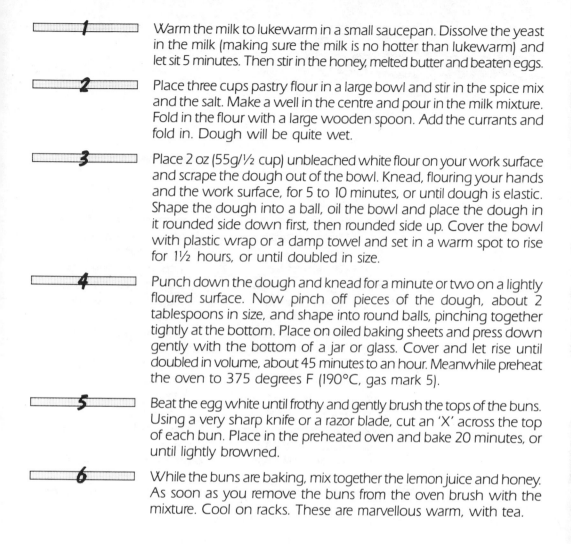

1 Warm the milk to lukewarm in a small saucepan. Dissolve the yeast in the milk (making sure the milk is no hotter than lukewarm) and let sit 5 minutes. Then stir in the honey, melted butter and beaten eggs.

2 Place three cups pastry flour in a large bowl and stir in the spice mix and the salt. Make a well in the centre and pour in the milk mixture. Fold in the flour with a large wooden spoon. Add the currants and fold in. Dough will be quite wet.

3 Place 2 oz (55g/½ cup) unbleached white flour on your work surface and scrape the dough out of the bowl. Knead, flouring your hands and the work surface, for 5 to 10 minutes, or until dough is elastic. Shape the dough into a ball, oil the bowl and place the dough in it rounded side down first, then rounded side up. Cover the bowl with plastic wrap or a damp towel and set in a warm spot to rise for 1½ hours, or until doubled in size.

4 Punch down the dough and knead for a minute or two on a lightly floured surface. Now pinch off pieces of the dough, about 2 tablespoons in size, and shape into round balls, pinching together tightly at the bottom. Place on oiled baking sheets and press down gently with the bottom of a jar or glass. Cover and let rise until doubled in volume, about 45 minutes to an hour. Meanwhile preheat the oven to 375 degrees F (190°C, gas mark 5).

5 Beat the egg white until frothy and gently brush the tops of the buns. Using a very sharp knife or a razor blade, cut an 'X' across the top of each bun. Place in the preheated oven and bake 20 minutes, or until lightly browned.

6 While the buns are baking, mix together the lemon juice and honey. As soon as you remove the buns from the oven brush with the mixture. Cool on racks. These are marvellous warm, with tea.

Black Bread

2 large loaves

Imperial (Metric)	American
1 heaped tablespoon Postum dissolved in 4 fl oz (120ml) hot water, or 4 fl oz (120ml) strong coffee	1 heaping tablespoon Postum dissolved in ½ cup hot water, or ½ cup strong coffee
2 tablespoons active dry yeast	2 tablespoons active dry yeast
¾ pint (500ml) lukewarm water	2 cups lukewarm water
2 fl oz (60ml) treacle	¼ cup dark molasses
1 teaspoon ground ginger	1 teaspoon ground ginger
4 oz (115g) wholemeal breadcrumbs	2 cups whole wheat breadcrumbs
½ lb (225g) unbleached white flour, plus more as necessary for kneading	2 cups unbleached white flour, plus more as necessary for kneading
4 tablespoons safflower oil	4 tablespoons safflower oil
2 teaspoons sea salt	2 teaspoons sea salt
¾ lb (340g) rye flour	3 cups rye flour
½ lb (225g) wholemeal flour	2 cups whole wheat flour
1 egg, beaten with 3 tablespoons of water for egg wash	1 egg, beaten with 3 tablespoons of water for egg wash
Poppy seeds for the topping	Poppy seeds for the topping

 Allow Postum or coffee to cool to lukewarm.

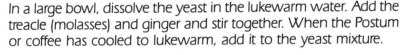 In a large bowl, dissolve the yeast in the lukewarm water. Add the treacle (molasses) and ginger and stir together. When the Postum or coffee has cooled to lukewarm, add it to the yeast mixture.

 Add the bread crumbs and unbleached flour, a cup at a time, and stir 100 times. Set this sponge aside in a warm place, covered with plastic wrap or a damp towel, to rise for 50 to 60 minutes.

 Fold in the oil and sea salt. Add the rye flour a cup at a time, and fold in. Begin adding the whole wheat flour. After one cup you should be able to turn out the dough, which will be sticky, onto

your kneading surface. Place the other cup of whole wheat flour on your kneading surface, scrape out the dough and begin to knead. Knead for 10 minutes, adding unbleached white flour as necessary.

5 When the dough is stiff and elastic, shape into a ball. Oil your bowl, then place the dough in it seam side down first, then seam side up. Cover and let rise in a warm place until doubled in bulk, about 1½ hours.

6 Punch down the dough and turn it out onto a lightly floured board. Divide into two equal pieces and shape the pieces into two long or round loaves. Make the loaves high, as the dough will spread out. Brush with oil and place on oiled cookie sheets or in baguette pans. Cover with a damp towel and let rise again for 30 minutes, or until nearly doubled in bulk.

7 Preheat the oven to 400 degrees F (200°C, gas mark 6). Brush the loaves with the egg wash and sprinkle with poppy seeds. Brush once more, slash and place in the preheated oven. Bake 40 to 45 minutes, brushing again with the egg wash halfway through the baking.

8 Remove from the baking sheet or pans and let cool on a rack.

Cheese and Mustard Bread

(1 loaf)

This bread is like a cheese sandwich with the cheese and mustard baked right into the loaf. When you toast it the fragrance of the mustard and cheese emerges and it smells like a grilled cheese sandwich. You can reduce the mustard by half if you want a more subtle flavour. This bread freezes well.

Imperial (Metric)	American
1 tablespoon active dry yeast	1 tablespoon active dry yeast
4 fl oz (120ml) lukewarm water	½ cup lukewarm water
4 fl oz (120ml) lukewarm milk	½ cup lukewarm milk
1 tablespoon mild-flavoured honey	1 tablespoon mild-flavored honey
1 teaspoon sea salt	1 teaspoon sea salt
1 teaspoon freshly ground black pepper	1 teaspoon freshly ground black pepper
1 egg, lightly beaten	1 egg, lightly beaten
1 teaspoon crushed rosemary	1 teaspoon crushed rosemary
8 tablespoons Dijon-style mustard	½ cup Dijon-style mustard
1 tablespoon grated onion	1 tablespoon grated onion
4 oz (115g) grated sharp Cheddar cheese	4 ounces grated sharp Cheddar cheese
¾ lb (340g) wholemeal flour	3 cups whole wheat flour
Up to 2 oz (55g) unbleached white flour for kneading	Up to ½ cup unbleached white flour for kneading
1 egg, beaten with 4 tablespoons water, for egg wash	1 egg, beaten with 4 tablespoons water, for egg wash

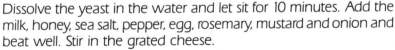

1 Dissolve the yeast in the water and let sit for 10 minutes. Add the milk, honey, sea salt, pepper, egg, rosemary, mustard and onion and beat well. Stir in the grated cheese.

2 Fold in the whole wheat flour a cup at a time. When the dough comes away from the sides of the bowl, place a half cup of flour on your kneading surface and turn out the dough. Knead for 10 minutes, or until the dough is smooth and elastic. Add more flour as necessary.

3 Oil the bowl and place the dough in it seam side up first, then seam side down. Let rise in a warm place for 30 minutes.

4 Punch the dough down, knead a few times and form into a loaf. Butter a loaf pan and place the dough in it, seam side up first, then seam side down. Cover loosely with plastic wrap and refrigerate overnight.

5 In the morning remove the dough from the refrigerator. Let it stand in a warm place for 45 minutes.

6 Preheat the oven to 350 degrees F (180°C, gas mark 4). Brush the loaf with egg wash, slash the top and bake in the preheated oven for 50 minutes. Remove from the pan and cool on a rack.

Buckwheat and Whole Wheat Bread with Cumin

(2 loaves)

Imperial (Metric)	American
For the Sponge	For the Sponge
1 tablespoon active dry yeast	1 tablespoon active dry yeast
¾ pint (500ml) lukewarm water	2 cups lukewarm water
1 cup natural, low-fat yogurt	1 cup plain, low-fat yogurt
2 tablespoons honey	2 tablespoons honey
1 tablespoon treacle	1 tablespoon molasses
½ lb (225g) unbleached white flour	2 cups unbleached white flour
½ lb (225g) wholemeal flour	2 cups whole wheat flour
For the Dough	For the Dough
1 tablespoon sea salt	1 tablespoon sea salt
4 tablespoons safflower oil	4 tablespoons safflower oil
2 heaped tablespoons cumin seeds	2 heaping tablespoons cumin seeds
4 oz (115g) buckwheat flour	1 cup buckwheat flour
4½ oz (130g) cracked wheat	¾ cup cracked wheat
¾ lb (340g) wholemeal flour, more as needed	3 cups whole wheat flour, more as needed
1 egg, for egg wash	1 egg, for egg wash

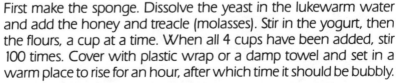

First make the sponge. Dissolve the yeast in the lukewarm water and add the honey and treacle (molasses). Stir in the yogurt, then the flours, a cup at a time. When all 4 cups have been added, stir 100 times. Cover with plastic wrap or a damp towel and set in a warm place to rise for an hour, after which time it should be bubbly.

Fold in the sea salt and oil, then the cumin, buckwheat flour and cracked wheat. Begin folding in the whole wheat flour, a cup at a time. As soon as you can scrape the dough out of the bowl, turn out onto a floured kneading surface. Flour your hands and knead for 10 minutes, or until the dough is stiff and elastic, adding flour as necessary.

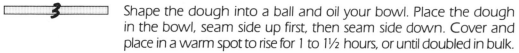

Shape the dough into a ball and oil your bowl. Place the dough in the bowl, seam side up first, then seam side down. Cover and place in a warm spot to rise for 1 to 1½ hours, or until doubled in bulk.

Punch down the dough and turn out onto a floured kneading surface. Knead a few times, then divide in two and form two loaves. Place in oiled bread pans and cover. Let rise 40 minutes to an hour, or until they rise above the tops of the pans.

Ten to fifteen minutes before the end of the rising time, preheat the oven to 375 degrees F (190°C, gas mark 5). Gently brush the tops of the loaves with beaten egg, slash with a razor blade or sharp knife, and place in the preheated oven.

Bake 50 to 60 minutes, or until golden brown and the loaves respond to tapping with a hollow, thumping sound. Remove from the pans and cool on a rack.

Swedish Limpa

(1 large, round loaf)
This sweet, subtly spiced bread is adapted from James Beard's recipe.

Imperial (Metric)	American
1 tablespoon active dry yeast	1 tablespoon active dry yeast
4 tablespoons lukewarm water	4 tablespoons lukewarm water
¾ pint (500ml) brown ale, heated to lukewarm	2 cups dark beer, heated to lukewarm
6 tablespoons honey	6 tablespoons honey
2 tablespoons melted butter or safflower oil	2 tablespoons melted butter or safflower oil
2 teaspoons sea salt	2 teaspoons sea salt
1 teaspoon ground cardamom	1 teaspoon ground cardamom
1 teaspoon crushed anise seeds	1 teaspoon crushed anise seeds
2 tablespoons grated orange peel	2 tablespoons grated orange peel
10 oz (285g) rye flour	2½ cups rye flour
4 oz (115g) wholemeal flour	1 cup whole wheat flour
½ lb (225g) unbleached white flour, plus more as necessary for kneading	2 cups unbleached white flour, plus more as necessary for kneading

1 Dissolve the yeast in the water in a large bowl and let sit for 5 minutes. Add the beer, honey, melted butter or oil, the sea salt, cardamom, anise seeds and orange peel and mix together well.

2 Mix together the flours and fold three cups into the yeast mixture. Stir 100 times, cover with plastic wrap or a damp towel, and set this sponge in a warm place for one hour.

3 Stir down the sponge and fold in a cup of the flour. Continue to add flour until you can turn out the dough, which will be sticky, onto a floured kneading surface. Knead for 10 to 15 minutes, adding only enough flour to make the dough workable. When the dough is stiff, form into a ball.

4 Rinse the bowl, oil it and place the dough in it seam side up first, and then seam side down. Let rise until doubled in bulk, about 1 hour.

5
Punch down the dough and shape into one large ball or two smaller balls. Place on an oiled baking sheet, brush with oil or melted butter, cover loosely with greaseproof (waxed) paper or plastic wrap, and refrigerate for 2 to 3 hours.

6
Remove from the refrigerator and let sit for 15 minutes while you preheat the oven to 375 degrees F (190°C, gas mark 5). Bake 1 hour for large loaf, 40 to 45 minutes for smaller loaves, or until the bread is golden brown and sounds hollow when tapped on the bottom. Cool on a rack.

Naans with Sweet Pine Nut-Raisin Filling

(6 large naans)

Naans are flat, yeasted breads which are traditionally baked in a Tandoori oven but still yield delicious results when baked under a grill (broiler).

These naans are stuffed with a sweet, anisy paste made with golden raisins, pine nuts and spices. Some of the paste is spread in the middle, and some on the top. They are great for breakfast as well as lunch or dinner.

Imperial (Metric)	American
For the Dough	**For the Dough**
2 tablespoons lukewarm water	2 tablespoons lukewarm water
2 teaspoons active dry yeast	2 teaspoons active dry yeast
6 fl oz (200ml) milk, warmed to lukewarm	¾ cup milk, warmed to lukewarm
1 egg, beaten	1 egg, beaten
2 teaspoons honey	2 teaspoons honey
4 tablespoons natural, low-fat yogurt	4 tablespoons plain, low-fat yogurt
2 tablespoons safflower oil	2 tablespoons safflower oil
1 teaspoon sea salt	1 teaspoon sea salt
1 teaspoon baking powder (optional)	1 teaspoon baking powder (optional)
4 oz (115g) unbleached white flour	1 cup unbleached white flour
2 oz (60g) chick pea flour	½ cup garbanzo flour
12 oz (340g) wholemeal flour Additional flour for dusting	3 cups whole wheat flour Additional flour for dusting
For the Filling	**For the Filling**
1½ cups sultanas	1½ cups golden raisins
½ cup pinenuts	½ cup pine nuts
1¼ teaspoons crushed anise seeds	1¼ teaspoons crushed anise seeds

½ teaspoon crushed cardamom seeds	½ teaspoon crushed cardamom seeds
½ cup natural low-fat yogurt	½ cup plain low-fat yogurt

1 Dissolve the yeast in the water in a cup.

2 In a large bowl combine the milk, egg, honey, yogurt, oil, sea salt and yeast mixture. Stir in the baking powder, then add the unbleached white flour and fold in. Fold in the chick pea (garbanzo) flour and begin folding in the whole wheat flour a cup at a time.

3 As soon as the dough is in a semblance of one piece, turn it out onto a generously floured board and begin to knead, adding flour as necessary. Knead for 10 minutes, or until the dough is elastic, and form into a ball. Clean and oil your bowl, then place the dough in it rounded side down first, then rounded side up. Cover with a damp towel and let rise for 1½ to 2 hours, or until doubled in bulk, in a warm place.

4 Meanwhile make the filling. Place the sultanas (golden raisins) in a bowl and pour on boiling water to cover. Let plump 15 minutes, then drain and pat dry with paper towels. Blend to a paste in a food processor or mash in a mortar and pestle. Add the pine nuts and spices and continue to mash together, but make sure the pine nuts retain some texture. Some can remain whole.

5 When the dough has risen, preheat the broiler. Brush three baking sheets with oil.

6 Punch down the dough and turn out onto a lightly floured work surface. Knead a few times, then divide into six equal pieces. Shape these into balls, then roll each one out to a teardrop shape so that they taper at the bottom and are about ¼ inch (½ cm) thick. Spread with 1 heaped tablespoon of the pine nut-raisin paste (there will be some left over, which you will spread on the top) and fold the narrow bottom half of the dough up over the top half. Fold the overlapping edges in and over and pinch together tightly. Place on the baking sheets, two on a sheet, cover with a damp towel and let rise 20 minutes.

7 These bake very quickly under the grill (broiler), and you have to watch them carefully. Place about 3 inches from the grill (broiler) and let bake for 1 minute. Check after one minute and if they aren't beginning to brown continue baking for a second minute. If they are beginning to brown, reduce heat slightly for the second minute. After two minutes they should be golden brown (leave, watching

Continued over page

carefully, up to another minute if they are not). Turn and cook for one minute on the other side. Now spread some of the remaining pine nut-raisin paste over the top of each naan and place under the grill (broiler) for another minute or two. Remove from the heat and serve hot. These can be reheated in the oven, wrapped in foil, and will keep several days in the refrigerator. You can also roll out the naans and keep the dough refrigerated, covered with plastic wrap, for up to a day.

These go very well with tea or for breakfast.

Naans with Spicy Chick Pea (Garbanso) Filling

(6 large naans)
These naans are almost like a pitta bread with the stuffing baked right in it. They are a high-protein meal in themselves.

Imperial (Metric)	American
For the Dough	For the Dough
2 tablespoons lukewarm water	2 tablespoons lukewarm water
2 teaspoons active dry yeast	2 teaspoons active dry yeast
6 fl oz (200ml) milk, warmed to lukewarm	¾ cup milk, warmed to lukewarm
1 egg, beaten	1 egg, beaten
2 teaspoons honey	2 teaspoons honey
4 tablespoons natural, low-fat yogurt	4 tablespoons plain, low-fat yogurt
2 tablespoons safflower oil	2 tablespoons safflower oil
1 teaspoon sea salt	1 teaspoon sea salt
1 teaspoon baking powder (optional)	1 teaspoon baking powder (optional)
4 oz (115g) unbleached white flour	1 cup unbleached white flour
2 oz (60g) chick pea (gram) flour	½ cup garbanzo flour
12 oz (340g) wholemeal flour	3 cups whole wheat flour
Additional flour for dusting	Additional flour for dusting

For the Filling	For the Filling
½ lb (225g) chick peas, cooked	2 cups garbanzos, cooked
4 fl oz (120ml) natural, low-fat yogurt	½ cup plain, low-fat yogurt
1 teaspoon crushed cumin seeds	1 teaspoon crushed cumin seeds
1 teaspoon crushed fennel seeds	1 teaspoon crushed fennel seeds
1 teaspoon crushed cardamom seeds	1 teaspoon crushed cardamom seeds
⅛ teaspoon cayenne pepper, or more to taste	⅛ teaspoon cayenne pepper, or more to taste
Sea salt and freshly ground pepper to taste	Sea salt and freshly ground pepper to taste

 Dissolve the yeast in the water in a cup.

 In a large bowl combine the milk, egg, honey, yogurt, oil, sea salt and yeast mixture. Stir in the baking powder, then add the unbleached white flour and fold in. Fold in the chick pea (garbanzo) flour and begin folding in the whole wheat flour a cup at a time.

 As soon as the dough is in a semblance of one piece, turn it out onto a generously floured board and begin to knead, adding flour as necessary. Knead for 10 minutes, or until the dough is elastic, and form into a ball. Clean and oil your bowl, then place the dough in it rounded side down first, then rounded side up. Cover with a damp towel and let rise for 1½ to 2 hours, or until doubled in bulk, in a warm place.

 Meanwhile make the filling. Mash the chick peas (garbanzos) in a mortar and pestle, or in a food processor or blender, and mix with the yogurt and spices, which you have crushed in a mortar and pestle or a spice mill. Season to taste with sea salt, cayenne and freshly ground pepper. It should be a little piquant and should have a pastelike consistency.

 When the dough has risen, preheat the grill (broiler). Brush three baking sheets with oil.

Punch down the dough and turn out onto a lightly floured work surface. Knead a few times, then divide into six equal pieces. Shape these into balls, then roll each one out to a teardrop shape so that they taper at the bottom and are about ¼-inch thick. Spread with 3 heaping tablespoons of the chick pea (garbanzo) paste and fold

Continued over page

the narrow bottom half of the dough up over the top half. Fold the overlapping edges in and over and pinch together tightly. Place on the baking sheets, two on a sheet, cover with a damp towel and let rise 20 minutes.

7

These bake very quickly under the grill (broiler), and you have to watch them carefully. Place about 3 inches from the grill (broiler) and let bake for 1 minute. Check after one minute and if they aren't beginning to brown continue baking for a second minute. If they are beginning to brown, reduce heat slightly for the second minute. After two minutes they should be golden brown (leave, watching carefully, up to another minute if they are not). Turn and repeat this process on the other side. Remove from the heat and serve hot. These can be reheated in the oven, wrapped in foil, and will keep several days in the refrigerator. You can also roll out the naans and keep the dough refrigerated, covered with plastic wrap, for up to a day.

These are large and filling and can be cut in half to serve or can even be cut into pieces to serve as hors d'oeuvres. The protein is complete, and they make a good main dish.

Boston Brown Bread with Ginger

(2 loaves)

This steamed dark bread is adapted from my version in *The Vegetarian Feast*. I've spiced up the original version with ground ginger.

Imperial (Metric)	American
4 oz (115g) rye flour	1 cup rye flour
5 oz (140g) stoneground yellow maize	1 cup stone-ground yellow cornmeal
4 oz (115g) wholemeal flour	1 cup whole wheat flour
2 teaspoons bicarbonate of soda	2 teaspoons baking soda
1 teaspoon sea salt	1 teaspoon sea salt
1 tablespoon ground ginger	1 tablespoon ground ginger
6 fl oz (200ml) treacle	¾ cup dark molasses
¾ pint buttermilk or natural low-fat yogurt	2 cups buttermilk or plain, low-fat yogurt
6 oz (170g) raisins	1 cup raisins

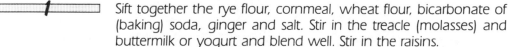 Sift together the rye flour, cornmeal, wheat flour, bicarbonate of (baking) soda, ginger and salt. Stir in the treacle (molasses) and buttermilk or yogurt and blend well. Stir in the raisins.

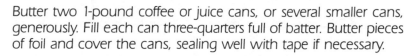 Butter two 1-pound coffee or juice cans, or several smaller cans, generously. Fill each can three-quarters full of batter. Butter pieces of foil and cover the cans, sealing well with tape if necessary.

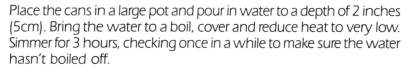 Place the cans in a large pot and pour in water to a depth of 2 inches (5cm). Bring the water to a boil, cover and reduce heat to very low. Simmer for 3 hours, checking once in a while to make sure the water hasn't boiled off.

Remove the cans from the pot, unmould and cool on a rack. If your bread seems too moist, place in a moderate oven for 10 minutes.

Banana Nut Bread

(1 loaf)

Imperial (Metric)	American
4 oz (115g) wholemeal flour	1 cup whole wheat flour
4 oz (115g) unbleached white flour	1 cup unbleached white flour
1 teaspoon bicarbonate of soda	1 teaspoon baking soda
1 teaspoon cinnamon	1 teaspoon cinnamon
½ teaspoon nutmeg	½ teaspoon nutmeg
½ teaspoon sea salt	½ teaspoon sea salt
4 tablespoons melted butter	4 tablespoons melted butter
4 fl oz (120ml) mild-flavoured honey	½ cup mild-flavored honey
1 teaspoon vanilla extract	1 teaspoon vanilla extract
2 eggs	2 eggs
3 medium-sized bananas, mashed	3 medium-sized bananas, mashed
4 tablespoons natural, low-fat yogurt	4 tablespoons plain, low-fat yogurt
5 oz (140g) chopped walnuts	1 cup chopped walnuts

1 Preheat the oven to 375 degrees F (190°C, gas mark 5). Butter an 8 × 5 × 3 inch (16 × 10 × 6cm) loaf pan.

2 Sift together the flours, bicarbonate of (baking) soda, spices and sea salt.

3 Beat together the melted butter, honey, vanilla, eggs, bananas and yogurt.

4 Quickly stir the wet ingredients into the dry (or vice versa). Fold in the chopped nuts. Turn into the prepared bread pan and bake in the preheated oven for 50 to 60 minutes, or until a cake tester comes out clean.

5 Remove from the oven and let cool in the pan for 10 minutes, then turn out onto a rack and cool completely.

Courgette (Zucchini) Bread

(1 loaf)

Imperial (Metric)	American
4 eggs	4 eggs
6 fl oz (200ml) safflower or vegetable oil	¾ cup safflower or vegetable oil
6 fl oz (200ml) mild-flavoured honey	¾ cup mild-flavored honey
2 teaspoons vanilla extract	2 teaspoons vanilla extract
1 tablespoon grated orange rind	1 tablespoon grated orange rind
½ lb (225g) grated courgettes	2 cups (½ pound) grated zucchini
½-lb (225g) wholemeal pastry flour	2 cups whole wheat pastry flour
2 teaspoons bicarbonate soda	2 teaspoons baking soda
1 teaspoon baking powder	1 teaspoon baking powder
½ teaspoon sea salt	½ teaspoon sea salt
2 teaspoons ground cinnamon	2 teaspoons ground cinnamon
1 teaspoon ground cloves	1 teaspoon ground cloves
1 teaspoon ground nutmeg	1 teaspoon ground nutmeg
½ teaspoon ground allspice	½ teaspoon ground allspice
5 oz (140g) shelled walnuts or pecans, chopped	1 cup shelled walnuts or pecans, chopped

1 Preheat the oven to 350 degrees F (180°C, gas mark 4). Butter a 9 × 5 inch (18 × 10cm) loaf pan.

2 Beat together the eggs, oil, honey and vanilla. Stir in courgettes (zucchini) and orange rind.

3 Sift together the flour, bicarbonate of (baking) soda, baking powder, sea salt and spices. Stir into liquid mixture and mix just until well blended. Fold in the nuts.

4 Pour into the prepared bread pan and bake in the preheated oven on the middle rack for 1 hour and 15 minutes, or until a tester comes out clean.

5 Cool for ten minutes in the pans, then reverse on a rack and cool completely. Wrap in plastic wrap and foil and let sit overnight so the flavours will develop. This makes a very nice tea or dessert bread.

Pain D'Epices

(1 loaf)

This recipe is from my *Herbs and Honey Cookery*. I can't leave it out of this collection of spice recipes. There are many versions of this bread, and this is just one of them.

Imperial (Metric)	American
4 oz (115g) unsalted butter or safflower oil	4 ounces unsalted butter or safflower oil
6 tablespoons strong-flavoured honey	6 tablespoons strong-flavored honey
2 tablespoons treacle	2 tablespoons molasses
6 fl oz (170ml) milk	¾ cup milk
1 egg, beaten	1 egg, beaten
1 tablespoon lemon juice	1 tablespoon lemon juice
½ lb (225g) wholemeal flour	2 cups whole wheat flour
2 oz (55g) rye flour	½ cup rye flour
1 teaspoon bicarbonate of soda	1 teaspoon baking soda
1½ tablespoons ground anise seeds	1½ tablespoons ground anise seeds
¼ teaspoon ground allspice	¼ teaspoon ground allspice
½ teaspoon ground cardamom	½ teaspoon ground cardamom
½ teaspoon ground coriander	½ teaspoon ground coriander
½ teaspoon grated nutmeg	½ teaspoon grated nutmeg
¼ teaspoon ground ginger	¼ teaspoon ground ginger
¼ teaspoon ground cloves	¼ teaspoon ground cloves
Pinch of sea salt	Pinch of sea salt

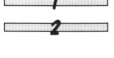

Preheat the oven to 375 degrees F (190°C, gas mark 5).

Cream together the butter or safflower oil, the honey and the treacle (molasses). Beat in the milk, egg and lemon juice.

Sift together the flours, soda, sea salt and spices. Stir into the liquid mixture and blend well.

Butter a loaf pan and line with buttered waxed or greaseproof paper. Spoon in the batter and bake in the preheated oven for 50 to 60 minutes, or until a tester comes out clean. Turn out onto a wire rack and remove the paper. Cool completely and wrap tightly in plastic wrap and foil. Let sit for several days before eating so that the spices can ripen. This will stay good for two weeks.

Cheese, Pepper and Mustard Muffins

(12 to 14 muffins)

Imperial (Metric)	American
¼ lb (115g) wholemeal flour	1 cup whole wheat flour
¼ lb (115g) unbleached white flour	1 cup unbleached white flour
½ teaspoon sea salt	½ teaspoon sea salt
2½ teaspoons baking powder	2½ teaspoons baking powder
2 teaspoons freshly ground black pepper	2 teaspoons freshly ground black pepper
2 eggs	2 eggs
4 tablespoons safflower oil or melted butter	¼ cup safflower oil or melted butter
2 teaspoons mild-flavoured honey	2 teaspoons mild-flavored honey
8 fl oz (225ml) milk	1 cup milk
2 tablespoons Dijon-style mustard	2 tablespoons Dijon-style mustard
4 oz (115g) grated Cheddar cheese	1 cup grated Cheddar or Monterry Jack cheese

 **1** Preheat the oven to 375 degrees F (190°C, gas mark 5). Butter muffin tins.

2 Sift together the flours, salt, pepper and baking powder.

3 Beat together the eggs, oil or melted butter, honey, milk and mustard. Stir in the cheese.

4 Quickly stir the wet ingredients into the dry and spoon into muffin tins. Bake 20 minutes in the preheated oven. Serve hot, or cool on racks.

Jalapeño Corn Muffins

(15 muffins)

Imperial (Metric)	American
7½ oz (200g) stone-ground yellow cornmeal	1¼ cups stone-ground yellow cornmeal
3 oz (85g) wholemeal flour	¾ cup whole wheat flour
2½ teaspoons baking powder	2½ teaspoons baking powder
½ teaspoon sea salt	½ teaspoon sea salt
1 egg	1 egg
4 tablespoons safflower oil or melted butter	4 tablespoons safflower oil or melted butter
1 tablespoon mild-flavoured honey	1 tablespoon mild-flavored honey
12 fl oz (340ml) milk	1½ cups milk
1 to 2 jalapeño chilli peppers, to taste, seeded and chopped	1 to 2 jalapeño chili peppers, to taste, seeded and chopped

1 Preheat the oven to 400 degrees F (200°C, gas mark 6). Butter muffin tins.

2 Sift together the cornmeal, flour, baking powder and sea salt.

3 In another bowl beat together the egg, oil or melted butter, the honey and the milk. Stir in the chopped jalapeños.

4 Quickly stir the wet ingredients into the dry, being careful not to stir too much. Spoon into muffin tins (this is a runny batter) and bake in a preheated oven for 20 minutes, or until firm and beginning to brown. Serve hot, or cool on racks.

Sweet Potato Muffins

16 muffins

Imperial (Metric)	American
4 oz (115g) unbleached white flour	1 cup unbleached white flour
4 oz (115g) wholemeal flour	1 cup whole wheat flour
1 tablespoon baking powder	1 tablespoon baking powder
1 teaspoon cinnamon	1 teaspoon cinnamon
½ teaspoon grated nutmeg	½ teaspoon grated nutmeg
¼ teaspoon sea salt	¼ teaspoon sea salt
¾ lb (340g) cooked, mashed sweet potatoes	¾ pound cooked, mashed sweet potatoes
4 tablespoons melted butter	4 tablespoons melted butter
4 fl oz (120ml) apple juice	½ cup apple juice
4 fl oz (120ml) mild-flavoured honey	½ cup mild-flavored honey
4 tablespoons fresh lime juice	4 tablespoons fresh lime juice
3 eggs	3 eggs
4 fl oz (120ml) milk or natural, low-fat yogurt	½ cup milk or plain, low-fat yogurt

Preheat the oven to 400 degrees F (200°C, gas mark 6). Butter muffin tins.

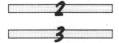

Sift together the flours, baking powder, sea salt and spices.

Beat together the sweet potatoes, melted butter, apple juice, honey, lime juice, eggs and milk or yogurt. Quickly stir into the dry ingredients. Spoon into muffin tins and bake for 25 to 30 minutes, or until beginning to brown. Cool on a rack or serve warm.

Pecan Rolls

(2 dozen)

Imperial (Metric)	American
6 oz (170g) raisins	1 cup raisins
Boiling water to cover the raisins	Boiling water to cover the raisins
8 fl oz (225ml) soya or cow's milk, scalded, cooled to lukewarm	1 cup soy or cow's milk, scalded and cooled to lukewarm
8 fl oz (225ml) lukewarm orange juice	1 cup lukewarm orange juice
1 tablespoon active dry yeast	1 tablespoon active dry yeast
6 tablespoons mild-flavoured honey	6 tablespoons mild-flavored honey
6 tablespoons safflower oil or melted butter	6 tablespoons safflower oil or melted butter
4 fl oz (120ml) natural, low-fat yogurt	½ cup plain, low-fat yogurt
2 tablespoons grated orange peel	2 tablespoons grated orange peel
1 teaspoon sea salt	1 teaspoon sea salt
1 teaspoon ground cardamom	1 teaspoon ground cardamom
½ teaspoon ground mace or nutmeg	½ teaspoon ground mace or nutmeg
4 tablespoons soya flour	4 tablespoons soy flour
½ lb (225g) unbleached white flour	2 cups unbleached white flour
¾ lb (340g) wholemeal flour, or as needed	3 cups whole wheat flour, or as needed
4 tablespoons additional melted butter	4 tablespoons additional melted butter
2 tablespoons additional honey	2 tablespoons additional honey
7 oz (200g) chopped pecans	1½ cups chopped pecans
Cinnamon	Cinnamon
For the Topping	For the Topping
6 tablespoons butter, melted	⅓ cup butter, melted
4 tablespoons honey, warmed with the butter	¼ cup honey, warmed with the butter
½ teaspoon cinnamon	½ teaspoon cinnamon
2 oz (55g) chopped pecans	½ cup chopped pecans

1   Soak the raisins in boiling water to cover for 15 minutes and then drain.

2   Dissolve the yeast in the milk and add the orange juice and honey. Let sit about 10 minutes.

3   Stir in the 6 tablespoons safflower oil or melted butter, the raisins, yogurt, orange peel, sea salt, spices and soya (soy) flour. Mix well and fold in the unbleached white flour, a cup at a time. Begin folding in the whole wheat flour, and when the dough comes away from the sides of the bowl, turn it out onto a floured surface. Dough will be sticky.

4   Knead 10 to 15 minutes, adding flour as necessary to the kneading surface. Shape into a ball.

5   Clean the bowl and oil it. Place the dough in it seam side down, then seam side up. Cover with plastic wrap or a damp towel and let the dough rise in a warm place for 1½ to 2 hours, or until double in bulk.

6   Punch down the dough, knead a few times and cut in two. Roll out each half into a large rectangle about ¼ inch (½cm) thick.

7   Melt the additional 4 tablespoons butter and the 2 tablespoons honey together over low heat. Brush the rectangles with this mixture and sprinkle generously with cinnamon. Spread ¾ cup of pecans evenly over each rectangle, and roll up lengthwise tightly like a jelly roll.

8   Cut each cylinder into rolls 1½ inches (3cm) thick. Butter muffin tins.

9   Melt together the butter and honey for the topping, and add the cinnamon. Brush the muffin tins with this mixture and sprinkle with a few chopped pecans. Place the cut pecan rolls in the tins. Cover loosely with plastic wrap and let rise 30 minutes, then refrigerate overnight. Retain the remaining butter/honey mixture for the completed rolls.

10   In the morning, preheat the oven to 350 degrees F (180°C, gas mark 4) and remove the rolls from the refrigerator. Let sit in a warm place for 30 minutes, then bake for 20 to 25 minutes, or until brown, in the preheated oven. Meanwhile heat the remaining butter/honey mixture.

11   Remove the pecan rolls from the oven, reverse onto a rack, brush the tops with the remaining butter and honey and allow to cool.

Yogurt Coffee Cake with Apple-Nut Filling

Imperial (Metric)	American
4 tablespoons unsalted butter	4 tablespoons unsalted butter
4 tablespoons safflower oil	4 tablespoons safflower oil
6 fl oz (200ml) mild-flavoured honey	¾ cup mild-flavored honey
3 eggs, beaten	3 eggs, beaten
12 fl oz (340ml) natural low-fat yogurt	1½ cups plain, low-fat yogurt
1 tablespoon vanilla extract	1 tablespoon vanilla extract
4 oz (115g) wholemeal pastry flour	1 cup whole wheat pastry flour
4 oz (115g) unbleached white flour	1 cup unbleached white flour
1 tablespoon baking powder	1 tablespoon baking powder
1 teaspoon cinnamon	1 teaspoon cinnamon
¼ teaspoon sea salt	¼ teaspoon sea salt
For the Filling	For the Filiing
3 medium-sized apples, peeled, cored and thinly sliced	3 medium-sized apples, peeled, cored and thinly sliced
2 tablespoons lemon juice	2 tablespoons lemon juice
1 tablespoon cinnamon	1 tablespoon cinnamon
½ teaspoon ground nutmeg	½ teaspoon ground nutmeg
½ teaspoon ground cloves	½ teaspoon ground cloves
4 oz (115g) chopped pecans or walnuts	¾ cup chopped pecans or walnuts

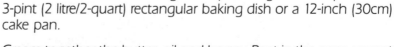 **1** Preheat the oven to 350 degrees F (180°C, gas mark 4). Butter a 3-pint (2 litre/2-quart) rectangular baking dish or a 12-inch (30cm) cake pan.

2 Cream together the butter, oil and honey. Beat in the eggs, yogurt and vanilla.

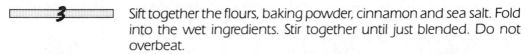

3   Sift together the flours, baking powder, cinnamon and sea salt. Fold into the wet ingredients. Stir together until just blended. Do not overbeat.

4   Toss the thinly sliced apples with the lemon juice, spices and chopped nuts.

5   Turn half the batter into the prepared pan. Layer the filling evenly over the batter. Top with the remaining batter.

6   Place in the preheated oven and bake 60 to 90 minutes, or until a tester when inserted in the middle comes out clean. Remove from the oven and cool on a rack for 30 minutes, then cut in wedges or squares and serve.

Pecan-Yogurt Coffee Cake

Imperial (Metric)	American
4 tablespoons unsalted butter	4 tablespoons unsalted butter
4 tablespoons safflower oil	4 tablespoons safflower oil
6 fl oz (200ml) mild-flavoured honey	¾ cup mild-flavored honey
3 eggs, beaten	3 eggs, beaten
12 fl oz (340ml) natural, low-fat yogurt	1½ cups plain, low-fat yogurt
1 tablespoon vanilla extract	1 tablespoon vanilla extract
4 oz (115g) wholemeal pastry flour	1 cup whole wheat pastry flour
4 oz (115g) unbleached white flour	1 cup unbleached white flour
1 tablespoon baking powder	1 tablespoon baking powder
¼ teaspoon sea salt	¼ teaspoon sea salt
For the Filling	For the Filling
10 oz (285g) chopped pecans or walnuts	2 cups chopped pecans or walnuts
2 oz (55g) raisins (optional)	⅓ cup raisins (optional)
1 tablespoon cinnamon	1 tablespoon cinnamon
½ teaspoon ground nutmeg	½ teaspoon ground nutmeg
½ teaspoon ground cloves	½ teaspoon ground cloves

1 Preheat the oven to 350 degrees F (180°C, gas mark 4). Butter a 3 pint (2 litre/2-quart) rectangular baking dish or a 12-inch (30cm) cake pan.

2 Cream together the butter, oil and honey. Beat in the eggs, yogurt and vanilla. Sift together the flours, baking powder and sea salt. Fold into the wet ingredients. Stir together until just blended. Do not overbeat. Mix together the nuts, optional raisins and the spices.

3 Turn half the batter into the prepared pan. Sprinkle the chopped nut-and-spice mixture in an even layer over the batter. Top with the remaining batter.

4 Place in the preheated oven and bake 60 to 90 minutes, or until a tester when inserted in the middle comes out clean. Remove from the oven and cool on a rack for 30 minutes, then cut in wedges or squares and serve.

2. Soups

Vegetable Stock

Makes 3 pints (2 litres/2 quarts)

Imperial (Metric)	American
3 pints (2 litres) water	2 quarts water
2 onions, quartered	2 onions, quartered
Cloves from 1 head garlic, peeled	Cloves from 1 head garlic, peeled
2 carrots, coarsely sliced	2 carrots, coarsely sliced
2 leeks, white part only, cleaned and coarsely sliced	2 leeks, white part only, cleaned and coarsely sliced
4 potatoes, scrubbed and quartered	4 potatoes, scrubbed and quartered
2 turnips, peeled and diced	2 turnips, peeled and diced
2 sticks celery, coarsely sliced	2 stalks celery, coarsely sliced
2 sprigs parsley	2 sprigs parsley
1 bay leaf	1 bay leaf
¼ teaspoon thyme	¼ teaspoon thyme
Sea salt to taste	Sea salt to taste
12 black peppercorns	12 black peppercorns
4 whole cloves	4 whole cloves

Combine all the ingredients in a soup pot and bring to a simmer. Cover, reduce heat and simmer one to two hours. Strain and discard the vegetables. This can be frozen and will last for several days in the refrigerator.

Easy Vegetable Bouillon

Makes 3 pints (2 litres/2 quarts).

Imperial (Metric)	American
3 pints (2 litres) water	2 quarts water
4 vegetable bouillon cubes (available in natural foods stores)	4 vegetable bouillon cubes (available in natural foods stores)
4 tablespoons soya sauce (more to taste)	4 tablespoons soy sauce (more to taste)

Simmer the above ingredients together until the bouillon cubes dissolve.

Ginger-Vegetable Stock

Makes 3 pints (2 litres/2 quarts).

Imperial (Metric)	American
3 pints (2 litres) water	2 quarts water
2 onions, quartered	2 onions, quartered
Cloves from 1 head garlic, peeled	Cloves from 1 head garlic, peeled
A 1-inch (2cm) piece of ginger, peeled and thinly sliced	A 1-inch piece of ginger, peeled and thinly sliced
2 carrots, coarsely sliced	2 carrots, coarsely sliced
2 leeks, white part only, cleaned and coarsely sliced	2 leeks, white part only, cleaned and coarsely sliced
4 potatoes, scrubbed and quartered	4 potatoes, scrubbed and quartered
2 turnips, peeled and diced	2 turnips, peeled and diced
2 sticks celery, coarsely sliced	2 stalks celery, coarsely sliced
2 sprigs parsley	2 sprigs parsley
1 bay leaf	1 bay leaf
¼ teaspoon thyme	¼ teaspoon thyme
Sea salt to taste	Sea salt to taste
12 black peppercorns	12 black peppercorns
4 whole cloves	4 whole cloves

Combine all the ingredients in a soup pot and bring to a simmer. Cover, reduce heat and simmer one to two hours. Strain and discard the vegetables. This can be frozen and will last for several days in the refrigerator.

Cream of Spinach Soup

Serves 4 to 6

Imperial (Metric)	American
1 tablespoon safflower or vegetable oil	1 tablespoon safflower or vegetable oil
1 medium-sized onion, chopped	1 medium-sized onion, chopped
2 cloves garlic, minced or put through a press	2 cloves garlic, minced or put through a press
1 teaspoon ground cumin	1 teaspoon ground cumin
¼ teaspoon ground cloves	¼ teaspoon ground cloves
¼ teaspoon ground nutmeg	¼ teaspoon ground nutmeg
¼ teaspoon freshly ground pepper	¼ teaspoon freshly ground pepper
1¼ pints (710ml) Regular or Ginger-Vegetable Stock or Bouillon (pages 59-61)	3 cups Regular or Ginger-Vegetable Stock or Bouillon (pages 59-61)
2 slices peeled fresh ginger, about ⅛ inch (¼cm) thick	2 slices peeled, fresh ginger, about ⅛ inch thick
2 lb (1 kilo) fresh spinach, stemmed and washed, or 3 10-oz (285g) packages frozen, thawed	2 pounds fresh spinach, stemmed and washed, or 3 10-ounce packages, frozen, thawed
3 oz (85g) cooked rice, or 1 medium potato, peeled and diced	½ cup cooked rice, or 1 medium potato, peeled and diced
Sea salt to taste	Sea salt to taste
½ pint (285ml) milk	1 cup milk
2 to 3 tablespoons double cream (to taste)	2 to 3 tablespoons heavy cream (to taste)
Juice of 1 lemon, or more, to taste	Juice of 1 lemon, or more, to taste
Additional pepper or cayenne pepper to taste	Additional pepper or cayenne pepper to taste
1 lemon, sliced, for garnish	1 lemon, sliced, for garnish
Natural low-fat yogurt for garnish	Plain, low-fat yogurt for garnish

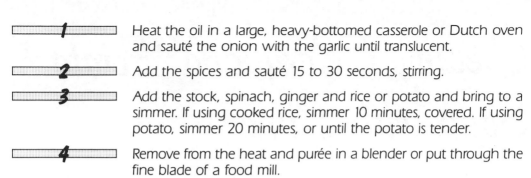

_1_ Heat the oil in a large, heavy-bottomed casserole or Dutch oven and sauté the onion with the garlic until translucent.

_2_ Add the spices and sauté 15 to 30 seconds, stirring.

_3_ Add the stock, spinach, ginger and rice or potato and bring to a simmer. If using cooked rice, simmer 10 minutes, covered. If using potato, simmer 20 minutes, or until the potato is tender.

_4_ Remove from the heat and purée in a blender or put through the fine blade of a food mill.

_5_ Return to the pot, add the milk and cream and sea salt to taste. Heat through, stirring. Adjust seasonings, adding more spices if you wish.

_6_ Just before serving, stir in the lemon juice. Serve garnished with thin slices of lemon and a dollop of yogurt.

Note: This soup is also nice cold. In this case, chill before you add the lemon juice. Stir in the lemon juice just before serving.

Creamy Celery and Potato Soup with Lime

Serves 8.

Imperial (Metric)	American
1 cinnamon stick, 3 inches (6cm) long, broken into pieces	1 cinnamon stick, 3 inches long, broken into pieces
6 whole cloves	6 whole cloves
3 white or green cardamom pods	3 white or green cardamom pods
1 teaspoon black peppercorns	1 teaspoon black peppercorns
1 tablespoon safflower or vegetable oil	1 tablespoon safflower or vegetable oil
2 medium onions, chopped	2 medium onions, chopped
1 large clove garlic, peeled and left whole	1 large clove garlic, peeled and left whole
2 teaspoons chopped fresh ginger	2 teaspoons chopped fresh ginger
1 lb (500g) celery, chopped, with leaves	1 pound celery, chopped, with leaves
¾ lb (340g) potatoes, peeled and diced	¾ pound potatoes, peeled and diced
¼ teaspoon turmeric	¼ teaspoon turmeric
2½ pints (1.5 litres) Regular or Ginger-Vegetable Stock (pages 59 and 61)	6 cups Regular or Ginger-Vegetable Stock (pages 59 and 61)
6 fl oz (200ml) milk	¾ cup milk
Sea salt to taste	Sea salt to taste
4 heaped tablespoons coriander leaves, minced	¼ cup firmly packed coriander leaves, minced
Juice of 1 large lime (more to taste)	Juice of 1 large lime (more to taste)
1 lime, sliced thin, for garnish	1 lime, sliced thin, for garnish

1 Tie the cinnamon stick, cloves, cardamom and peppercorns loosely in a 6-inch (15 cm) square piece of cheesecloth. Using a rolling pin, pound the packet lightly to break up the spices.

2 Heat the oil in a large, heavy-bottomed soup pot or casserole and sauté the onion until tender. Add the garlic, ginger, celery, potato and turmeric and sauté another couple of minutes, stirring. Add the vegetable stock and the spices in their cheesecloth bag and bring to a boil.

3 Reduce heat, cover and simmer 30 minutes. Remove the cheesecloth bag and purée the soup in a blender or through a food mill.

4 Return the soup to the pot and add the milk. Heat through, add sea salt to taste and stir in the coriander (alternatively, you can blend the coriander with the soup when you purée it). Stir in the lime juice and serve at once, garnishing with thin slices of lime.

Mulligatawny I

Serves 6 to 8.

Imperial (Metric)	American
2 tablespoons safflower or vegetable oil, or butter	2 tablespoons safflower or vegetable oil, or butter
1 tablespoon curry powder	1 tablespoon curry powder
1 onion, minced	1 onion, minced
2 teaspoons minced fresh ginger	2 teaspoons minced fresh ginger
2 tart apples, peeled and diced	2 tart apples, peeled and diced
2 carrots, minced	2 carrots, minced
3 oz (85g) raw peanuts	½ cup raw peanuts
2 green peppers, seeded and chopped	2 green peppers, seeded and chopped
3 pints (2 litres) Regular or Ginger-Vegetable Stock (pages 59 and 61)	2 quarts Regular or Ginger-Vegetable Stock (pages 59 and 61) or water
4 whole cloves	4 whole cloves
2 oz (55g) almonds, coarsely ground in a blender	½ cup almonds, coarsely ground in a blender
1 tablespoon mild-flavoured honey	1 tablespoon mild-flavored honey
2 tablespoons shredded coconut	2 tablespoons shredded coconut
3 oz (85g) raisins	½ cup raisins
1 teaspoon ground mace or nutmeg	1 teaspoon ground mace or nutmeg
Sea salt and freshly ground pepper to taste	Sea salt and freshly ground pepper to taste
3 tomatoes, peeled and chopped	3 tomatoes, peeled and chopped
9 oz (255g) cooked long-grain brown rice	1½ cups cooked long-grain brown rice
1 additional apple, sliced thin, for garnish	1 additional apple, sliced thin, for garnish

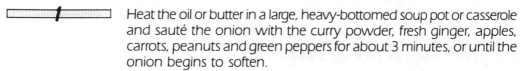

1 Heat the oil or butter in a large, heavy-bottomed soup pot or casserole and sauté the onion with the curry powder, fresh ginger, apples, carrots, peanuts and green peppers for about 3 minutes, or until the onion begins to soften.

2 Add the vegetable stock or water, the cloves, almonds, honey, coconut, raisins, mace or nutmeg, sea salt, pepper and tomatoes and bring to a simmer. Cover and simmer over low heat for 30 minutes.

3 Remove half the soup and purée in a blender. Return to the pot and stir together well.

4 Heat through, adjust seasonings and stir in the cooked brown rice. Serve, topping each bowl with thinly sliced apple.

Mulligatawny II

Serves 6 to 8.

Imperial (Metric)	American
1 onion, finely chopped	1 onion, finely chopped
2 carrots, finely chopped	2 carrots, finely chopped
2 sticks celery, finely chopped	2 stalks celery, finely chopped
2 oz (55g) chopped mushrooms	1 cup chopped mushrooms
1 lb (500g) aubergine, peeled and diced	1 pound eggplant, peeled and diced
2 turnips, chopped	2 turnips, chopped
2 slices peeled ginger root	2 slices peeled ginger root
2½ pints (1.5 litres) Regular Vegetable Stock (page 59)	6 cups Regular Vegetable Stock (page 59)
2 large cloves garlic, peeled, left whole	2 large cloves garlic, peeled, left whole
2 sprigs coriander	2 sprigs coriander
¼ teaspoon ground black pepper	¼ teaspoon ground black pepper
2 teaspoons curry powder, plus more to taste	2 teaspoons curry powder, plus more to taste
Sea salt to taste	Sea salt to taste
8 fl oz (225ml) natural low-fat yogurt	1 cup plain low-fat yogurt
3 tablespoons minced fresh coriander	3 tablespoons minced fresh coriander

1 Combine all the vegetables, the ginger root, stock, the two sprigs coriander, curry powder and the ground black pepper and bring to a simmer. Simmer 1 hour, covered.

2 Purée the soup in a blender or through a food mill. Return to the pot and adjust seasonings, adding salt to taste.

3 Heat through, and just before serving whisk in the yogurt and minced fresh coriander.

Spicy Apple Soup

Serves 6 to 8.

Imperial (Metric)	American
2½ pints (1.5 litres) water	1½ quarts water
2 lb (1 kilo) tart apples, peeled, cored and sliced	2 pounds tart apples, peeled, cored and sliced
6 oz (170g) raisins or sultanas	1 cup dark or golden raisins
1½ teaspoons freshly grated nutmeg	1½ teaspoons freshly grated nutmeg
2 teaspoons ground cinnamon	2 teaspoons ground cinnamon
¼ to ½ teaspoon ground cloves, to taste	¼ to ½ teaspoon ground cloves, to taste
½ teaspoon ground allspice	½ teaspoon ground allspice
3 to 4 tablespoons mild-flavoured honey	3 to 4 tablespoons mild-flavored honey
4 oz (115g) rolled or flaked oats	½ cup rolled or flaked oats
Juice of ½ to 1 lemon, to taste	Juice of ½ to 1 lemon, to taste
2 tablespoons brandy	2 tablespoons brandy
8 fl oz (200ml) natural, low-fat yogurt	1 cup plain low-fat yogurt
Thin slices of lemon and additional nutmeg for garnish	Thin slices of lemon and additional nutmeg for garnish

1 Combine the water, apples, raisins, spices and honey in a large soup pot or casserole and bring to a boil. Add the oats, cover and reduce heat. Simmer for 45 minutes.

2 Stir in the lemon juice, brandy and half the yogurt. Taste and adjust seasonings, adding more spices or honey if you wish.

3 Serve, garnishing each bowl with a dollop of yogurt, a thin slice of lemon and a discreet sprinkle of nutmeg.

Delicate Lentil Soup

Serves 4.

Imperial (Metric)	American
1 inch (2cm) ball tamarind	1 inch ball tamarind
2 fl oz (60ml) boiling water	¼ cup boiling water
1 onion, chopped	1 onion, chopped
2 cloves garlic, minced or put through a press	2 cloves garlic, minced or put through a press
1 tablespoon safflower oil	1 tablespoon safflower oil
8 oz (225g) yellow lentils	1 cup yellow lentils
1½ pints (1 litre) water	4 cups water
1 lb (500g) tomatoes (fresh or tinned), chopped	2 cups chopped tomatoes (fresh or canned)
1 teaspoon treacle	1 teaspoon molasses
1 tablespoon ground coriander	1 tablespoon ground coriander
1 teaspoon ground cumin	1 teaspoon ground cumin
¼ teaspoon ground black pepper	¼ teaspoon ground black pepper
Cayenne to taste	Cayenne to taste
Sea salt to taste	Sea salt to taste
3 tablespoons chopped fresh coriander	3 tablespoons chopped fresh coriander
Natural low-fat yogurt for garnish	Plain low-fat yogurt for garnish

Place the tamarind in a bowl and cover with ¼ cup boiling water. Let sit while you begin the soup.

Heat the safflower oil in a large, heavy-bottomed soup pot or casserole and add the onion and garlic. Sauté until the onion is tender and add the lentils, water, tomatoes, treacle (molasses), spices and sea salt to taste. Bring to a boil. Reduce heat, cover and simmer 30 minutes, or until the lentils are tender.

Meanwhile mash the tamarind pulp with the back of a spoon or with your fingers and strain the liquid through a fine strainer, making sure to squeeze out all the liquid. Add the juice to the lentils.

4 When the lentils are tender, purée in a blender. Then press through a fine strainer. Discard the pulp or save for another purpose, such as a bean spread. Return the liquid to the heat and heat through. Adjust seasonings and serve, garnishing each bowl with a dollop of plain, low-fat yogurt and a sprinkling of chopped fresh coriander.

Cabbage-Apple Soup

Serves 4 to 6.

Imperial (Metric)	American
1 tablespoon safflower oil	1 tablespoon safflower oil
1 large onion, chopped	1 large onion, chopped
2 cloves garlic, minced or put through a press	2 cloves garlic, minced or put through a press
1 teaspoon cinnamon	1 teaspoon cinnamon
¼ teaspoon turmeric	¼ teaspoon turmeric
¼ teaspoon ground cloves	¼ teaspoon ground cloves
1 to 2 teaspoons curry powder, to taste	1 to 2 teaspoons curry powder, to taste
1 lb (500g) red or green cabbage, shredded	1 pound red or green cabbage, shredded
2½ pints (1.5 litres) water or Ginger or Regular Vegetable Stock (pages 59 and 61)	6 cups water or Ginger or Regular Vegetable Stock (pages 59 and 61)
1 to 2 tablespoons soya sauce (optional)	1 to 2 tablespoons soy sauce (optional)
Sea salt to taste	Sea salt to taste
2 tart apples, cored and sliced	2 tart apples, cored and sliced
8 fl oz (225ml) natural low-fat yogurt	1 cup plain low-fat yogurt

For Garnish	For Garnish
4 fl oz (120ml) additional yogurt	½ cup additional yogurt
½ additional apple, sliced thin and tossed with lemon juice	½ additional apple, sliced thin and tossed with lemon juice
Freshly ground pepper to taste	Freshly ground pepper to taste

1 Heat the safflower oil in a heavy-bottomed soup pot or Dutch oven and sauté the onion and garlic over medium heat until the onion begins to soften. Add the spices and sauté another 2 to 3 minutes, stirring. Add the cabbage and sauté another 5 minutes, stirring. Add the water or stock, the soya (soy) sauce and salt to taste. Bring to a boil, reduce heat, cover and simmer 30 minutes.

2 Add the apples and continue to simmer another 15 to 20 minutes. Taste and adjust seasoning, adding more salt or curry powder to taste. Remove from the heat, cool a minute and stir in the yogurt and freshly ground pepper to taste. Serve, topping each bowl with a spoonful of yogurt and a few slices of apple.

Cabbage Soup Chinoise

Serves 4 to 6.

Imperial (Metric)	American
2 pints (1.1 litres) Ginger Vegetable Stock (page 61), or Vegetable Bouillon	5 cups Ginger-Vegetable Stock (page 61) or Vegetable Bouillon
1 lb (500g) Chinese cabbage, shredded	1 pound Chinese cabbage, shredded
6 spring onions, thinly sliced	6 green onions, thinly sliced
4 tablespoons soya sauce	4 tablespoons soy sauce
2 tablespoons sherry	2 tablespoons sherry
1 teaspoon grated fresh ginger	1 teaspoon grated fresh ginger
½ to 1 lb (250-500g) tofu, cut in cubes or slivers (optional)	½ to 1 pound tofu, cut in cubes or slivers (optional)
1 tablespoon cornflour, dissolved in 2 tablespoons water	1 tablespoon cornstarch dissolved in 2 tablespoons water
2 tablespoons sesame seeds and chopped fresh coriander for garnish	2 tablespoons sesame seeds and chopped fresh coriander for garnish

1 Place the stock in a large soup pot and bring to a simmer. Add the Chinese cabbage and spring (green) onions and simmer 5 minutes, or until the cabbage is cooked through but still has some texture.

2 Stir in the soya (soy) sauce, sherry, ginger and tofu and heat through for 5 minutes. Stir in the cornflour (cornstarch) dissolved in the water and heat through, stirring, until the soup is thickened. Serve at once, garnishing each serving with sesame seeds and chopped fresh coriander.

Soupe au Coriandre

Imperial (Metric)	American
1 tablespoon olive oil	1 tablespoon olive oil
1 onion, chopped	1 onion, chopped
2 cloves garlic, minced or put through a press	2 cloves garlic, minced or put through a press
1 teaspoon ground cumin	1 teaspoon ground cumin
1½ teaspoons paprika	1½ teaspoons paprika
1 32-oz (900g) tin tomatoes, chopped, with juice	1 32-ounce can tomatoes, chopped, with juice
1½ pints (1 litre) water	4 cups water
4 tablespoons tomato purée	4 tablespoons tomato paste
2 whole bunches coriander	2 whole bunches coriander
Sea salt and freshly ground pepper to taste	Sea salt and freshly ground pepper to taste
¾ oz (20g) vermicelli	½ cup vermicelli
Pinch of cayenne	Pinch of cayenne
Juice of 1 lime, or more, to taste	Juice of 1 lime, or more, to taste

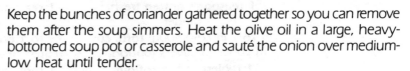

1 Keep the bunches of coriander gathered together so you can remove them after the soup simmers. Heat the olive oil in a large, heavy-bottomed soup pot or casserole and sauté the onion over medium-low heat until tender.

2 Add the garlic, cumin and paprika, sauté a minute, and add the tomatoes and their juice, the water, the tomato purée (paste), coriander and sea salt and freshly ground pepper to taste. Bring to a simmer, cover and simmer 30 minutes.

3 Remove the soup from the heat. Take out the coriander bunches and discard, and put the soup through a food mill. Return to the heat, bring back to a simmer and add the vermicelli. Cook until al dente, adjust seasonings and stir in the lime juice. Serve at once.

Guacamole Soup

Serves 6 to 8.

Imperial (Metric)	American
1¼ pints (710ml) tomato juice	3 cups tomato juice
1 tomato, peeled and quartered	1 tomato, peeled and quartered
1 small onion, quartered	1 small onion, quartered
1 jalapeno or serrano pepper, seeds removed	1 jalapeno or serrano pepper, seeds removed
1 to 2 cloves garlic, to taste, peeled	1 to 2 cloves garlic, to taste, peeled
3 large or 4 small ripe avocados, peeled and pitted	3 large or 4 small ripe avocados, peeled and pitted
2 fl oz (60ml) lemon juice (juice of 1 large lemon)	¼ cup lemon juice (juice of 1 large lemon)
1 teaspoon ground cumin	1 teaspoon ground cumin
½ teaspoon chilli powder (more to taste)	½ teaspoon chili powder (more to taste)
Sea salt to taste	Sea salt to taste
¾ pint (500ml) natural low-fat yogurt	2 cups plain low-fat yogurt
Additional yogurt and chopped fresh coriander for garnish	Additional yogurt and chopped fresh coriander for garnish

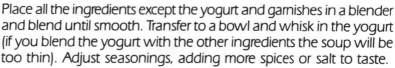

Place all the ingredients except the yogurt and garnishes in a blender and blend until smooth. Transfer to a bowl and whisk in the yogurt (if you blend the yogurt with the other ingredients the soup will be too thin). Adjust seasonings, adding more spices or salt to taste.

Cover and refrigerate for several hours before serving. Serve garnished with a dollop of yogurt and chopped fresh coriander.

Potato-Cheese Soup with Cumin

Serves 6 to 8.

Imperial (Metric)	American
1 tablespoon safflower oil, vegetable oil or butter	1 tablespoon safflower oil, vegetable oil or butter
4 leeks, white part only, cleaned well and sliced thin	4 leeks, white part only, cleaned well and sliced thin
1 tablespoon cumin seeds, slightly crushed	1 tablespoon cumin seeds, slightly crushed
2 lb (1 kilo) russet potatoes, unpeeled and diced	2 pounds russet potatoes, unpeeled and diced
1½ pints (1 litre) Regular Vegetable Stock (page 59)	1 quart Regular Vegetable Stock (page 59)
¾ pint (425ml) milk	2 cups milk
Sea salt and freshly ground pepper to taste	Sea salt and freshly ground pepper to taste
6 oz (170g) sharp Cheddar or Gruyère cheese, grated	6 ounces sharp Cheddar or Gruyère cheese, grated
2 eggs, beaten	2 eggs, beaten

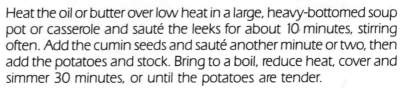

1 Heat the oil or butter over low heat in a large, heavy-bottomed soup pot or casserole and sauté the leeks for about 10 minutes, stirring often. Add the cumin seeds and sauté another minute or two, then add the potatoes and stock. Bring to a boil, reduce heat, cover and simmer 30 minutes, or until the potatoes are tender.

2 With the back of your spoon, mash some of the potatoes against the side of the pot to thicken the soup a little. Stir in the milk, heat through and add sea salt and freshly ground pepper to taste (remembering that the cheese will be salty).

3 Beat the eggs and stir in the cheese. Ladle some of the hot soup into the mixture, stir together, then stir the entire mixture into the soup. Heat through but do not boil, and serve.

Curried Cauliflower Soup

Serves 4 to 6.

Imperial (Metric)	American
1 onion, chopped	1 onion, chopped
1 clove garlic, minced or put through a press	1 clove garlic, minced or put through a press
1 tablespoon safflower oil	1 tablespoon safflower oil
1 to 2 teaspoons curry powder, to taste	1 to 2 teaspoons curry powder, to taste
½ to 1 teaspoon ground cumin, to taste	½ to 1 teaspoon ground cumin, to taste
¼ teaspoon turmeric	¼ teaspoon turmeric
1 small head, or about 1½ lb (750g), cauliflower, broken into florets	1 small head, or about 1½ pounds, cauliflower, broken into florets
2 pints (1.25 litres) Regular or Ginger Vegetable Stock (pages 59 and 61) or Bouillon	5 cups Regular or Ginger-Vegetable Stock (pages 59 and 61) or Bouillon
1 small potato, peeled and diced	1 small potato, peeled and diced
Sea salt to taste	Sea salt to taste
8 fl oz (225ml) natural, low-fat yogurt	1 cup plain, low-fat yogurt
1 teaspoon cornflour	1 teaspoon cornstarch
Freshly ground pepper to taste	Freshly ground pepper to taste
Lemon juice to taste (optional)	Lemon juice to taste (optional)

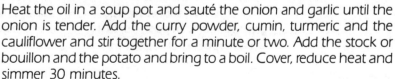

1 Heat the oil in a soup pot and sauté the onion and garlic until the onion is tender. Add the curry powder, cumin, turmeric and the cauliflower and stir together for a minute or two. Add the stock or bouillon and the potato and bring to a boil. Cover, reduce heat and simmer 30 minutes.

2 Purée in a blender or food processor in batches. Return to the pot and adjust seasonings, adding salt, pepper and curry powder or cumin to taste. Heat through.

3 Stir together the yogurt and cornflour (starch) and whisk into the soup. Heat through and serve.

Hot and Sour Soup

Serves 6.

Imperial (Metric)	American
6 dried Chinese mushrooms	6 dried Chinese mushrooms
3 pints (2 litres) Ginger Vegetable Stock (page 61)	2 quarts Ginger-Vegetable Stock (page 61)
6 spring onions, sliced, white and green parts separated	6 green onions, sliced, white and green parts separated
½ lb (250g) tofu, slivered	½ pound tofu, slivered
2 tablespoons dry sherry or Chinese rice wine	2 tablespoons dry sherry or Chinese rice wine
2 fl oz (60ml) cider vinegar or Chinese rice wine vinegar (more to taste)	¼ cup cider vinegar or Chinese rice wine vinegar (more to taste)
2 to 3 tablespoons soya sauce, preferably tamari, or more to taste	2 to 3 tablespoons soy sauce, preferably tamari, or more to taste
2 tablespoons cornflour or arrowroot	2 tablespoons cornstarch or arrowroot
4 tablespoons water	4 tablespoons water
2 eggs, beaten	2 eggs, beaten
1 large carrot, cut in 2-inch matchsticks	1 large carrot, cut in 2-inch matchsticks
1 stick celery or bok choy, cut in 2-inch (5cm) matchsticks	1 stalk celery or bok choy, cut in 2-inch matchsticks
3 oz (85g) cucumber, cut in matchsticks	½ cup cucumber, cut in matchsticks
¼ to ½ teaspoon freshly ground black pepper, to taste	¼ to ½ teaspoon freshly ground black pepper, to taste
2 tablespoons chopped fresh coriander	2 tablespoons chopped fresh coriander

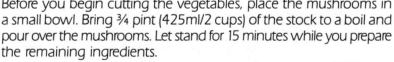

1 Before you begin cutting the vegetables, place the mushrooms in a small bowl. Bring ¾ pint (425ml/2 cups) of the stock to a boil and pour over the mushrooms. Let stand for 15 minutes while you prepare the remaining ingredients.

2 Place the remaining ginger-vegetable stock in a large soup pot or casserole. Drain the mushrooms and retain the soaking liquid. Strain this through a cheesecloth or coffee filter and add it to the stock. Cut the mushrooms in slivers and add them to the stock, along with the white part of the spring (green) onions. Simmer 5 minutes and add the tofu. Simmer 5 more minutes and stir in the sherry, vinegar and tamari soya (soy) sauce.

3 Dissolve the cornflour (starch) or arrowroot in the water. Stir this into the soup and bring to a gentle boil and cook, stirring, until the soup thickens, about 3 minutes.

4 Drizzle the beaten eggs into the simmering soup, stirring with a fork or chopstick so that the eggs form shreds. Remove the soup from the heat, stir in the pepper, taste and adjust vinegar, soya (soy) sauce and pepper.

5 Distribute carrots, bok choy or celery, the cucumber and spring (green) onion tops among the bowls and ladle in the soup. Sprinkle a little fresh coriander on each bowlful and serve at once, passing additional pepper and vinegar so people can adjust the hot and sour to their tastes.

Sopa de Tortilla

Serves 6 to 8.

Imperial (Metric)	American
3 chillies pasillas	3 chilies pasillas
2 tablespoons safflower oil	2 tablespoons safflower oil
½ onion, minced	½ onion, minced
4 cloves garlic, minced or put through a press	4 cloves garlic, minced or put through a press
1 tablespoon olive oil	1 tablespoon olive oil
2½ pints (1.5 litres) Regular Vegetables Stock (page 59)	6 cups Regular Vegetable Stock (page 59)
2 tomatoes, peeled, seeded and puréed	2 tomatoes, peeled, seeded and puréed
4 tablespoons tomato purée	4 tablespoons tomato paste
Pinch of cayenne	Pinch of cayenne
Additional safflower or vegetable oil	Additional safflower or vegetable oil
12 stale corn tortillas, cut in strips	12 stale corn tortillas, cut in strips
3 tablespoons chopped fresh coriander, plus more for garnish	3 tablespoons chopped fresh coriander, plus more for garnish
Sea salt and freshly ground pepper to taste	Sea salt and freshly ground pepper to taste
2 oz (55g) Gruyère cheese, grated	2 ounces Gruyère cheese, grated
2 eggs, beaten	2 eggs, beaten

1 Heat 2 tablespoons safflower oil in a heavy-bottomed frying pan and fry the chillies pasillas until crisp. Remove from the heat and when cool enough to handle, crumble, discard seeds and set aside.

2 Heat the olive oil in a heavy-bottomed soup pot or casserole and add the onion and garlic. Cook over medium heat until the onion is tender. Add the puréed tomatoes and the tomato purée (paste). Cook over low heat for 8 to 10 minutes, and add the vegetable stock. Stir together well, add the cayenne and bring to a simmer. Cover and simmer over low heat for 30 minutes.

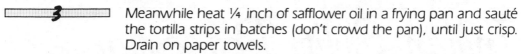 **3**

Meanwhile heat ¼ inch of safflower oil in a frying pan and sauté the tortilla strips in batches (don't crowd the pan), until just crisp. Drain on paper towels.

4

Shortly before serving the soup stir in the fried tortilla strips. Simmer for a minute or two, then add the coriander and sea salt and freshly ground pepper to taste.

5

Put some crumbled fried chillies pasillas in each bowl. Bring the soup to a boil and stir in the eggs. They should cook at once. Immediately spoon the soup into the bowls, top with cheese and a little more coriander if you wish, and serve.

Indian Split Pea Soup

Serves 4.

The flavour of this subtle, beautifully coloured soup is greatly enhanced by the lemon juice which you sprinkle on each bowl just before serving.

Imperial (Metric)	American
1 tablespoon black peppercorns	1 tablespoon black peppercorns
12 cloves	12 cloves
1 bay leaf, crushed	1 bay leaf, crushed
1 tablespoon safflower or vegetable oil, or butter	1 tablespoon safflower or vegetable oil, or butter
1 small onion, minced	1 small onion, minced
1 teaspoon mustard seeds	1 teaspoon mustard seeds
½ lb (250g) split peas, washed and picked over	½ pound split peas, washed and picked over
½ teaspoon turmeric	½ teaspoon turmeric
2 pints (1.25 litres) Plain or Ginger-Vegetable Stock (pages 59 and 61) or water	5 cups Plain or Ginger-Vegetable Stock (pages 59 and 61) or water
Sea salt and freshly ground pepper to taste	Sea salt and freshly ground pepper to taste
2 tablespoons milk or cream (optional)	2 tablespoons milk or cream (optional)
Juice of ½ lemon	Juice of ½ lemon
1 lemon, cut in wedges, for garnish	1 lemon, cut in wedges, for garnish
Croûtons, for garnish	Croûtons, for garnish
Natural low-fat yogurt for garnish (optional)	Plain low-fat yogurt for garnish (optional)

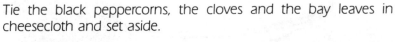

1 Tie the black peppercorns, the cloves and the bay leaves in cheesecloth and set aside.

2 Heat the oil in a heavy-bottomed soup pot or casserole and sauté the onion with the mustard seeds over medium heat until the onion is tender. Add the split peas, the turmeric, the stock or water, salt to taste and the spices in their cheesecloth bag. Bring to a boil, reduce heat and simmer 45 minutes to an hour, or until the peas are tender.

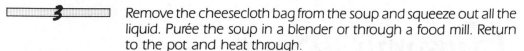

3 Remove the cheesecloth bag from the soup and squeeze out all the liquid. Purée the soup in a blender or through a food mill. Return to the pot and heat through.

4 Correct seasonings, adding salt and freshly ground pepper to taste, and stir in the optional milk or cream. Serve, sprinkling fresh lemon juice over each bowl and garnishing with lemon wedges, croûtons and optional plain low-fat yogurt.

'Hummus' Soup

Serves 6.

Since I love all the flavours of hummus, the spread made with chick peas (garbanzos), lemon, garlic, olive oil and tahini, I decided to see if they would translate into a soup. They did. This tastes best if served the day after it's made.

Imperial (Metric)	American
½ lb (250g) chick peas, washed, picked over and soaked overnight	½ pound garbanzos, washed, picked over and soaked overnight
2½ pints (1.5 litres) water	6 cups water
½ teaspoon turmeric	½ teaspoon turmeric
1 teaspoon ground cumin	1 teaspoon ground cumin
½ teaspoon ground coriander	½ teaspoon ground coriander
Pinch of saffron	Pinch of saffron
1 teaspoon, or more to taste, sea salt	1 teaspoon, or more to taste, sea salt
2 large cloves garlic (more to taste), peeled	2 large cloves garlic (more to taste), peeled
Juice of 2 lemons (2 to 3 oz, or 60 to 90ml lemon juice, to taste)	Juice of 2 lemons (¼ to ⅔ cup lemon juice, to taste)
5 to 6 tablespoons sesame tahini (to taste)	5 to 6 tablespoons sesame tahini (to taste)
8 fl oz (225ml) natural low-fat yogurt, plus additional for garnish	1 cup plain low-fat yogurt, plus additional for garnish
Additional lemon wedges for garnish	Additional lemon wedges for garnish

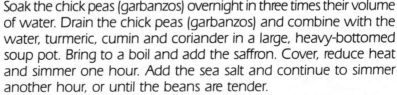

1 Soak the chick peas (garbanzos) overnight in three times their volume of water. Drain the chick peas (garbanzos) and combine with the water, turmeric, cumin and coriander in a large, heavy-bottomed soup pot. Bring to a boil and add the saffron. Cover, reduce heat and simmer one hour. Add the sea salt and continue to simmer another hour, or until the beans are tender.

2 Blend the soup to a smooth purée in a blender or food processor, along with the garlic, lemon juice and sesame tahini. Pour back into the pot and whisk in the yogurt. Thin out, if you wish, with water or additional yogurt. Taste and adjust seasonings. Heat through and serve, topping each bowl with a spoonful of yogurt and a sprinkling of lemon juice.

Rich Saffron Soup

Serves 6 to 8.
This soup had an unbelievably beautiful colour. The almonds and pine nuts give it a great texture, but if you want a lighter soup you may omit them.

Imperial (Metric)	American
3 pints (2 litres) Regular Vegetable Stock (page 59)	2 quarts Regular Vegetable Stock (page 59)
½ lb (250g) tofu, cut in slivers	½ pound tofu, cut in slivers
1 oz (30g) almonds, blanched and cut in slivers	1 ounce almonds, blanched and cut in slivers
½ oz (15g) pine nuts	½ ounce pine nuts
Pinch of cinnamon	Pinch of cinnamon
2 to 4 fl oz (60 to 120ml) dry sherry, to taste	¼ to ½ cup dry sherry, to taste
½ teaspoon imported saffron threads	½ teaspoon imported saffron threads
2 egg yolks	2 egg yolks
4 fl oz (120ml) double cream (or use milk enriched with 1 to 2 tablespoons spray-dried milk)	½ cup heavy cream (or use milk enriched with 1 to 2 tablespoons spray-dried milk)

1 Heat the vegetable stock in a soup pot or casserole and add the tofu, almonds and pine nuts. Simmer 5 minutes and add the sherry, saffron and cinnamon. Simmer 10 to 15 minutes. The broth will become very fragrant.

2 Beat the egg yolks and cream or enriched milk together in a bowl. Add a ladleful of the hot soup, stirring. Remove the soup from the heat and stir in the egg yolk mixture. Serve at once, or heat through, being careful not to boil, and serve.

Tomato-Lentil Rasam

Serves 4 to 6.

A 'rasam' is a highly seasoned South Indian broth made from the liquid which rises to the top when lentils, tomatoes and spices are cooked. This recipe is based on Julie Sahni's in *Classic Indian Cooking* (William Morrow and Co., NY, 1980). The 'Delicate Lentil Soup' on page 70 is a thicker, less spicy version of this rasam.

Imperial (Metric)	American
6 oz (170g) yellow lentils (toovar dal), washed and picked over	1 cup yellow lentils (toovar dal), washed and picked over
1 teaspoon turmeric	1 teaspoon turmeric
1 lb (500g) chopped tomatoes, fresh or canned	1 pound chopped tomatoes, fresh or canned
6 cloves garlic, peeled	6 cloves garlic, peeled
A 1-inch (2cm) ball of tamarind pulp (substitute juice of 1 lemon if you can't find tamarind)	A 1-inch ball of tamarind pulp (substitute juice of 1 lemon if you can't find tamarind)
1 teaspoon ground cumin	1 teaspoon ground cumin
¼ teaspoon black pepper	¼ teaspoon black pepper
⅛ to ¼ teaspoon cayenne pepper (to taste)	⅛ to ¼ teaspoon cayenne pepper (to taste)
1 tablespoon ground coriander	1 tablespoon ground coriander
1 teaspoon honey or treacle	1 teaspoon honey or molasses
Sea salt to taste	Sea salt to taste
1 tablespoon safflower or vegetable oil	1 tablespoon safflower or vegetable oil
1 teaspoon black mustard seeds	1 teaspoon black mustard seeds
⅛ teaspoon ground asafoetida (optional)	⅛ teaspoon ground asafoetida (optional)
2 to 3 tablespoons chopped fresh coriander	2 to 3 tablespoons chopped fresh coriander

Combine the lentils and 4 cups of water in a large saucepan and bring to a boil. Cover, reduce heat and simmer for about 35 minutes, or until the lentils are tender. Stir occasionally to prevent sticking.

2 Meanwhile place the tamarind pulp in a bowl and pour on 2 fl oz (60ml/¼ cup) boiling water. Let sit for 15 minutes. Strain the liquid into a bowl through a fine strainer, mashing the tamarind pulp against the sides of the strainer in order to extrude the maximum amount of juice.

3 While the lentils are simmering and the tamarind soaking, purée the tomatoes and garlic with 4 fl oz (120ml/½ cup) cold water and the turmeric, cumin, coriander, black pepper and cayenne in a blender or food processor. Set aside.

4 When the lentils are tender, purée in a blender, food processor or through a food mill, and return to the pot. Blend in 3 cups hot water with a whisk, mix thoroughly and allow the mixture to sit, undisturbed, for 15 minutes. A broth will accumulate at the top, and this is the broth you want. Pour off the broth and add enough water to measure 4½ cups. Transfer the lentil purée that remains to a bowl and save for another purpose. Return the broth to the pot and stir in the blended tomatoes and spices, the molasses or honey, the tamarind juice and sea salt to taste. Bring to a boil, reduce heat and simmer, partially covered, over low heat for 15 minutes. Remove from the heat.

5 Heat the oil over high heat in a small frying pan, and when it is very hot carefully add the mustard seeds. Keep a lid handy to protect yourself from spluttering oil. As soon as the seeds stop spluttering and turn grey—which will only take a few seconds—transfer the contents of the pan to the soup, recover the soup and let sit another 15 minutes.

6 To serve the soup, reheat to simmering, stirring, adjust salt and cayenne, stir in the coriander and serve.

Velvet Corn Soup with Green Chilli

Serves 4.

Imperial (Metric)	American
1 lb (500g) corn kernels, fresh or thawed frozen	3 cups corn kernels, fresh or thawed frozen
12 fl oz (340ml) milk (whole or low-fat)	1½ cups milk (whole or low-fat)
1 tablespoon mild-flavoured honey	1 tablespoon mild-flavored honey
1 tablespoon safflower, peanut or vegetable oil	1 tablespoon safflower, peanut or vegetable oil
3 spring onions with tops, sliced on the diagonal	3 green onions with tops, sliced on the diagonal
1 to 2 hot green chilli peppers, to taste, seeded and thinly sliced	1 to 2 hot green chili peppers, to taste, seeded and thinly sliced
1 teaspoon minced fresh ginger	1 teaspoon minced fresh ginger
1¼ pints (710ml) Regular or Ginger-Vegetable Stock (pages 59 and 61)	3 cups Regular or Ginger-Vegetable Stock (pages 59 and 61)
2 tablespoons good quality sherry or Chinese rice wine	2 tablespoons good quality sherry or Chinese rice wine
Sea salt to taste	Sea salt to taste
½ teaspoon sesame oil, (optional)	½ teaspoon sesame oil, (optional)
A generous amount of freshly ground white or black pepper	A generous amount of freshly ground white or black pepper
1 tablespoon cornflour	1 tablespoon cornstarch
2 tablespoons water	2 tablespoons water
2 egg whites, lightly beaten	2 egg whites, lightly beaten
3 tablespoons chopped fresh coriander	3 tablespoons chopped fresh coriander

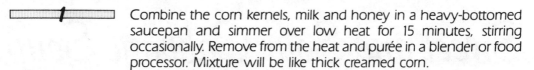

1 Combine the corn kernels, milk and honey in a heavy-bottomed saucepan and simmer over low heat for 15 minutes, stirring occasionally. Remove from the heat and purée in a blender or food processor. Mixture will be like thick creamed corn.

2 Heat the oil in a heavy-bottomed saucepan or casserole and add the spring (green) onions, chilli peppers and ginger. Sauté, stirring for 1 minute, and add the vegetable stock, corn purée, sherry, optional sesame oil and pepper. Mix together well. Bring to a simmer and simmer 5 minutes.

3 Dissolve the cornflour (cornstarch) in the water and stir into the soup. Cook, stirring, until the soup thickens, about 3 minutes. Remove from the heat and adjust seasonings.

4 Beat the egg whites until frothy and slowly drizzle them into the soup while you stir with a fork or wooden spoon so they cook in delicate threads. Ladle into warm bowls, garnish with chopped fresh coriander and serve at once.

Sweet and Sour Cabbage Soup

Serves 4 to 6.

This is a vegetarian version of the enticing 'Jewish Sweet and Sour Soup' in Richard Sax's *Cooking Great Meals Every Day* (Random House, 1982).

Imperial (Metric)	American
2 tablespoons safflower or vegetable oil	2 tablespoons safflower or vegetable oil
2 medium onions, sliced	2 medium onions, sliced
1 medium-sized cabbage, cored and cut in strips	1 medium-sized cabbage, cored and cut in strips
3 oz (85g) sultanas	½ cup golden raisins
Juice of 2 small or medium lemons (about 3 fl oz, or 90ml), more to taste	Juice of 2 small or medium lemons (about ⅓ cup) more to taste
2 tablespoons mild-tasting honey	2 tablespoons mild-tasting honey
2 cloves garlic, minced or put through a press	2 cloves garlic, minced or put through a press
Sea salt to taste	Sea salt to taste
2 teaspoons Hungarian paprika	2 teaspoons Hungarian paprika
¼ teaspoon ground cloves	¼ teaspoon ground cloves
1 2 lb (1 kilo) can tomatoes, with their liquid	1 2-pound can tomatoes, with their liquid
1½ pints (1 litre) water or Regular Vegetable Stock (page 59)	4 cups water or Regular Vegetable Stock (page 59)
2 tablespoons soya sauce	2 tablespoons soy sauce
2 slices dark pumpernickle bread, diced	2 slices dark pumpernickle bread, diced
Freshly ground black pepper to taste	Freshly ground black pepper to taste
Pinch of cayenne, (optional)	Pinch of cayenne, (optional)
Natural low-fat yogurt for garnish	Plain low-fat yogurt for garnish

1 Heat the oil over medium-low heat in a large, heavy-bottomed soup pot or casserole and add the onions. Sauté, stirring often, until the onions are soft, about 10 minutes.

2 Meanwhile prepare the cabbage and combine the raisins, lemon juice and honey in a small bowl.

3 Add the garlic, cabbage and salt to the pot with the sautéed onions, stir together well, cover and sauté, stirring from time to time, for about 4 minutes.

4 Add the paprika, cloves and tomatoes and stir together well. Add the water or vegetable stock, soya (soy) sauce, more salt to taste, the raisin/lemon juice mixture and the bread and bring to a simmer. Cover and simmer for 45 minutes to an hour, stirring from time to time.

5 Taste and adjust seasonings, adding freshly ground pepper to taste and a pinch of cayenne if you wish. Serve, garnishing each bowl with plain low-fat yogurt.

Piquant Chick Pea Soup

Serves 6.

Imperial (Metric)	American
1 lb (500g) chick peas, picked over, washed and soaked overnight	1 pound garbanzos, picked over, washed and soaked overnight
1 large onion, chopped	1 large onion, chopped
3 large cloves garlic (more to taste), minced or put through a press	3 large cloves garlic (more to taste), minced or put through a press
1 tablespoon olive oil	1 tablespoon olive oil
2 pints (1.25 litres) water	5 cups water
1 lb tomatoes, fresh or canned, chopped	1 pound tomatoes, fresh or canned, chopped
4 tablespoons tomato purée	4 tablespoons tomato paste
1 rind of Parmesan cheese	1 rind of Parmesan cheese
1 bay leaf	1 bay leaf
1 small, dried, hot red pepper, such as cayenne	1 small, dried, hot red pepper, such as cayenne
½ teaspoon thyme	½ teaspoon thyme
½ teaspoon oregano	½ teaspoon oregano
Sea salt and freshly ground pepper to taste	Sea salt and freshly ground pepper to taste
Chopped fresh parsley for garnish	Chopped fresh parsley for garnish

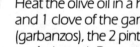 Combine the soaked chick peas (garbanzos) with 2½ pints (1.5 litres/6 cups) water, bring to a boil, reduce heat and simmer, covered, for one hour. Drain and set aside.

Heat the olive oil in a heavy-bottomed soup pot and sauté the onion and 1 clove of the garlic until the onion is tender. Add the chick peas (garbanzos), the 2 pints (1.25 litres/5 cups) water, the tomatoes, tomato purée (paste), Parmesan rind, bay leaf and hot red pepper and bring to a boil. Reduce heat, cover and simmer one to two hours, or until the beans are tender. Add the thyme, oregano, sea salt and pepper to taste, and cayenne and more garlic if you wish, and continue to simmer another 20 minutes. Serve garnished with chopped fresh parsley.

Almond Soup

Serves 4 to 6.

This soup is from my cookbook *The Vegetarian Feast*. Each spice is distinctive, yet the overall flavour of the soup is subtle. It is a rich soup with great texture.

Imperial (Metric)	American
1½ pints (1 litre) Regular or Ginger-Vegetables Stock (pages 59 and 61)	1 quart Regular or Ginger-Vegetable Stock (pages 59 and 61)
½ lb (250g) whole almonds, blanched	2 cups whole almonds, blanched
1 medium onion, chopped	1 medium onion, chopped
1 tablespoon butter or safflower oil	1 tablespoon butter or safflower oil
Grated rind of 1 to 2 lemons, to taste	Grated rind of 1 to 2 lemons, to taste
½ teaspoon ground cardamom	½ teaspoon ground cardamom
½ teaspoon caraway seeds	½ teaspoon caraway seeds
Sea salt and freshly ground pepper to taste	Sea salt and freshly ground pepper to taste
¾ pint (500ml) milk	2 cups milk
1 teaspoon lemon juice	1 teaspoon lemon juice
6 oz (170g) cooked, long-grain brown rice	1 cup cooked, long-grain brown rice
3 oz (85g) currants	½ cup currants
Freshly grated nutmeg to taste	Freshly grated nutmeg to taste

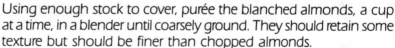

1   Using enough stock to cover, purée the blanched almonds, a cup at a time, in a blender until coarsely ground. They should retain some texture but should be finer than chopped almonds.

2   Heat the butter or oil in a heavy-bottomed soup pot or casserole and sauté the onion until tender. Add the almonds, remaining stock, the grated lemon peel, the cardamom, caraway seeds, sea salt and pepper. Cover and simmer gently for 30 minutes, stirring occasionally.

3   Carefully add the milk and lemon juice and correct seasonings. Add the rice and currants and simmer very gently for another 10 minutes. Grate some nutmeg over the top and serve, or chill and serve cold, grating additional nutmeg over each serving.

Peach Soup

Serves 6 to 8.

This recipe is also in my *Herb and Honey Cookery*. It is such a good example of a summer soup that makes the most of sweet spices that I couldn't resist including it in this collection.

Imperial (Metric)	American
3 lb (1.5 kilos) fresh, ripe peaches	3 pounds fresh, ripe peaches
3 to 4 tablespoons mild-flavoured honey, to taste	3 to 4 tablespoons mild-flavored honey, to taste
8 fl oz (225ml) orange juice	1 cup orange juice
3 tablespoons peach brandy or marsala	3 tablespoons peach brandy or marsala
3 tablespoons lemon or lime juice (more to taste)	3 tablespoons lemon or lime juice (more to taste)
¾ teaspoon cinnamon	¾ teaspoon cinnamon
½ teaspoon freshly grated nutmeg	½ teaspoon freshly grated nutmeg
¼ teaspoon ground ginger	¼ teaspoon ground ginger
½ teaspoon ground cardamom	½ teaspoon ground cardamom
½ to 1 teaspoon vanilla, to taste	½ to 1 teaspoon vanilla, to taste
2 pints (1.25 litres) buttermilk	5 cups buttermilk
2 oz (60g) slivered almonds, for garnish	½ cup slivered almonds, for garnish

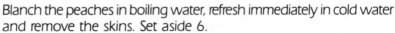

1 Blanch the peaches in boiling water, refresh immediately in cold water and remove the skins. Set aside 6.

2 Pit the remaining peaches and combine with the honey, orange juice, brandy or marsala, the lemon or lime juice, spices and vanilla. Purée in a blender or food processor. Transfer to a large bowl and stir in the buttermilk.

3 Slice the peaches you set aside and add to the soup. Cover and chill several hours.

4 Adjust seasonings and serve, garnishing each bowl with slivered almonds.

3. Vegetables

Cauliflower à la Saffron

Serves 4.

Imperial (Metric)	American
1 large head cauliflower, broken into florets (cut the florets in half or quarters if very large)	1 large head cauliflower, broken into florets (cut the florets in half or quarters if very large)
1¼ pints (750ml) water	3 cups water
¼ teaspoon saffron	¼ teaspoon saffron
¼ teaspoon sea salt (more to taste)	¼ teaspoon sea salt (more to taste)
2 tablespoons butter	2 tablespoons butter
2 tablespoons wholemeal pastry flour	2 tablespoons whole wheat pastry flour

1 Bring 8 fl oz (225ml/1 cup) of the water to a boil. Place the saffron in a small bowl and pour on the boiling water. Let steep for 10 to 15 minutes.

2 Bring the remaining water to a boil in a saucepan. Add the saffron water, sea salt and the cauliflower. Cover and cook 10 minutes. Drain and retain the cooking liquid, which you will use for a sauce.

3 In a heavy-bottomed saucepan melt the butter over medium heat. Add the flour and stir together well with a wooden spoon. Cook, stirring, for a minute or two. Now whisk in the liquid from the cauliflower. Bring to a boil, stirring all the while, and reduce heat. Stir until the sauce reaches the desired thickness. Add more salt to taste and freshly ground pepper, toss with the cauliflower, heat through and serve.

Aubergine (Eggplant) and Red Peppers with Fragrant Spices

The aubergine (eggplant) will have an almost puréed consistency in this marvellously perfumed dish. The strips of sweet red pepper lend a beautiful contrast of colours.

Imperial (Metric)	American
3 lb (1.5 kilos) aubergine, cut in half lengthwise	3 pounds eggplant, cut in half lengthwise
1 tablespoon flour	1 tablespoon flour
2 to 3 tablespoons safflower or vegetable oil, as needed	2 to 3 tablespoons safflower or vegetable oil, as needed
1 large onion, sliced thin	1 large onion, sliced thin
1 sweet red pepper, seeded and cut in lengthwise strips	1 sweet red pepper, seeded and cut in lengthwise strips
2 tablespoons minced fresh ginger	2 tablespoons minced fresh ginger
4 cloves garlic, minced or put through a press	4 cloves garlic, minced or put through a press
1½ teaspoons ground cumin	1½ teaspoons ground cumin
1½ teaspoons ground mace or nutmeg	1½ teaspoons ground mace or nutmeg
¾ teaspoon ground cinnamon	¾ teaspoon ground cinnamon
1 teaspoon Mughal Garam Masala (see page 25)	1 teaspoon Mughal Garam Masala (see page 25)
1 teaspoon paprika	1 teaspoon paprika
Cayenne pepper to taste	Cayenne pepper to taste
¾ pint (425ml) natural low-fat yogurt	2 cups plain low-fat yogurt
Sea salt to taste	Sea salt to taste
Milk as needed	Milk as needed

1 Preheat the oven to 450 degrees F (220°C, gas mark 7). Oil baking sheets. Score the halved aubergines (eggplants) once or twice, down to but not through the skin. Place cut side down on the baking sheets and bake 15 minutes, or until the skins begin to shrivel. (Meanwhile, prepare remaining ingredients.) Remove the aubergines (eggplants) from the oven and allow to cool. When cool enough to handle, scoop out from the skin, cut in dice and toss in a bowl with 1 tablespoon flour.

2 Heat the oil over medium heat in a large, wide, preferably nonstick frying pan and add the onion. Sauté until golden, about 5 to 10 minutes, and add the red pepper, garlic and ginger. Cook, stirring, for about 2 minutes, and stir in the spices. Cook for about 30 seconds, and add the aubergine (eggplant) and more oil (about a tablespoon) if necessary. Turn up the heat and brown the aubergine (eggplant), stirring constantly, for about 5 minutes.

3 Add half the yogurt, stir together, reduce heat and simmer the mixture for 15 minutes, stirring frequently. If the mixture sticks, add a little milk.

4 Taste and adjust the spices, adding sea salt to taste and more hot pepper if you wish. Remove from the heat, stir in the remaining yogurt, and serve with hot, cooked grains.

Spicy Aubergine (Eggplant) and Mangetout (Snow) Peas with Miso

Serves 6.

Imperial (Metric)	American
½ lb (250g) mangetout peas, trimmed	½ pound snow peas, trimmed
4 tablespoons hatcho miso	4 tablespoons hatcho miso
3 tablespoons water	3 tablespoons water
1 tablespoon mild-flavoured honey	1 tablespoon mild-flavored honey
1 teaspoon sesame oil	1 teaspoon sesame oil
1 medium-sized aubergine, peeled and diced small	1 medium-sized eggplant, peeled and diced small
2 tablespoons safflower or vegetable oil	2 tablespoons safflower or vegetable oil
2 cloves garlic, minced or put through a press	2 cloves garlic, minced or put through a press
2 teaspoons minced or grated fresh ginger	2 teaspoons minced or grated fresh ginger
8 spring onions, both white part and green, sliced	8 green onions, both white part and green, sliced
½ teaspoon hot red pepper flakes, or 1 small dried red pepper, crumbled, seeds removed	½ teaspoon hot red pepper flakes, or 1 small dried red pepper, crumbled, seeds removed

 Steam the peas for 5 to 10 minutes, to taste. Refresh under cold water and set aside.

 In a small bowl mix together the miso, water, honey and sesame oil. Set aside.

3 Heat the oil in a wok or a large, heavy-bottomed frying pan and add the aubergine (eggplant). Sauté for 5 minutes, stirring. Add the garlic and ginger and sauté another 10 minutes, stirring. Add the miso mixture and continue to stir-fry for another 3 to 5 minutes, then add the onions and pepper flakes or crumbled pepper and cook, stirring, until the onions and aubergine (eggplant) are tender. If necessary add a little more oil or 2 to 3 tablespoons water. Add the mangetout (snow) peas, toss together well, heat through and serve over hot, cooked grains.

Nutty Aubergine (Eggplant) and Potato Curry

Serves 6 to 8.

Imperial (Metric)	American
1½ lb (750g) aubergine, cut in half lengthwise	1½ pounds eggplant, cut in half lengthwise
2 tablespoons butter, safflower oil or vegetable oil	2 tablespoons butter, safflower oil or vegetable oil
1 medium sized onion, sliced	1 medium sized onion, sliced
½ lb (250g) potatoes, diced	½ pound potatoes, diced
1 clove garlic, minced or put through a press	1 clove garlic, minced or put through a press
1 teaspoon minced fresh ginger, or ¼ teaspoon dried	1 teaspoon minced fresh ginger, or ¼ teaspoon dried
1 tablespoon curry powder	1 tablespoon curry powder
1½ oz (45g) peanuts, almonds or sunflower seeds	¼ cup peanuts, almonds or sunflower seeds
3 oz (85g) raisins	½ cup raisins
8 fl oz (225ml) buttermilk or natural yogurt	1 cup buttermilk or plain yogurt
Sea salt and freshly ground pepper to taste	Sea salt and freshly ground pepper to taste
2 tablespoons chopped fresh coriander	2 tablespoons chopped fresh coriander

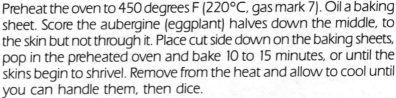

1   Preheat the oven to 450 degrees F (220°C, gas mark 7). Oil a baking sheet. Score the aubergine (eggplant) halves down the middle, to the skin but not through it. Place cut side down on the baking sheets, pop in the preheated oven and bake 10 to 15 minutes, or until the skins begin to shrivel. Remove from the heat and allow to cool until you can handle them, then dice.

2   Meanwhile steam the potatoes until crisp-tender, 10 to 15 minutes.

3   Heat the butter or oil in a heavy-bottomed frying pan or wok and add the onion, garlic and ginger. Sauté over medium-low heat for a minute or two, then add the curry powder. Sauté gently for about 15 minutes, stirring.

 **4**

Add the steamed potato and aubergine (eggplant), the raisins and nuts, more oil or butter if necessary, and sauté, stirring, for another 10 minutes. Add sea salt and freshly ground pepper to taste, remove from the heat, cool a moment and stir in the yogurt or buttermilk and the chopped, fresh coriander. Serve over hot, cooked grains.

Spicy Potatoes in Yogurt Gravy

Serves 8.

Imperial (Metric)	American
2 lb (1 kilo) new or red waxy potatoes, cut in large chunks	2 pounds new or red waxy potatoes, cut in large chunks
2 tablespoons safflower, sunflower or light vegetable oil	2 tablespoons safflower or light vegetable oil
2 onions, finely chopped	2 onions, finely chopped
1 tablespoon minced fresh ginger root	1 tablespoon minced fresh ginger root
2 teaspoons ground cumin	2 teaspoons ground cumin
2 teaspoons ground coriander	2 teaspoons ground coriander
1 teaspoon turmeric	1 teaspoon turmeric
¼ teaspoon cayenne	¼ teaspoon cayenne
1 teaspoon Mughal Garam Masala (page 25)	1 teaspoon Mughal Garam Masala (page 25)
1 lb (500g) chopped or puréed tomatoes, fresh or canned	1 pound chopped or puréed tomatoes, fresh or canned
12 fl oz (340ml) natural low-fat yogurt	1½ cups plain low-fat yogurt
Sea salt to taste	Sea salt to taste

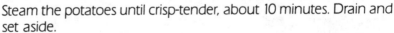

1 Steam the potatoes until crisp-tender, about 10 minutes. Drain and set aside.

2 Have the spices measured out and ready, right next to the stove. Heat the oil in a large, heavy-bottomed casserole or lidded frying pan and add the onions. Stir-fry, stirring constantly, for 10 minutes over medium-low heat or until they are beginning to be light brown. Add the ginger and fry for an additional ½ minute (add more oil if necessary), then add all the spices and stir together for another 30 seconds. Add the potatoes, tomatoes, half the yogurt and salt to taste, and bring to a boil. Reduce heat and simmer gently, covered, for about 30 minutes, or until the potatoes are tender. Stir from time to time to prevent sticking.

3

Remove from the heat, let sit a minute and stir in the remaining yogurt. Adjust salt and serve.

Note: This is best made a few hours or a day before and reheated gently.

Spicy Potatoes in Gravy

Serves 4

This dish is somewhere between a thick soup and a vegetable dish. I love the warming flavours. I serve it as a vegetable course, but in bowls. You could also serve it over rice.

Imperial (Metric)	American
1½ lb (750g) new or red waxy potatoes, diced	1½ pounds new or red waxy potatoes, diced
3 tablespoons safflower, sunflower or light vegetable oil	3 tablespoons safflower or light vegetable oil
1 teaspoon black mustard seeds	1 teaspoon black mustard seeds
2 teaspoons yellow split peas (channa dal, optional)	2 teaspoons yellow split peas (channa dal, optional)
2 tablespoons minced fresh ginger	2 tablespoons minced fresh ginger
1 to 2 green chillies, seeded and sliced, or ¼ teaspoon cayenne (optional)	1 to 2 green chillies, seeded and sliced, or ¼ teaspoon cayenne (optional)
1 tablespoon ground coriander	1 tablespoon ground coriander
1 teaspoon turmeric	1 teaspoon turmeric
½ teaspoon paprika	½ teaspoon paprika
2 onions, chopped	2 onions, chopped
Sea salt to taste	Sea salt to taste
4 tablespoons chopped fresh coriander	4 tablespoons chopped fresh coriander
Juice of 1 lemon, or more, to taste	Juice of 1 lemon, or more, to taste

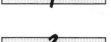 Steam the potatoes until tender, about 20 minutes. Drain and refresh under cold water, and set aside.

 Have the spices measured out and ready, right next to the stove.

Heat the oil over medium heat in a large, heavy-bottomed saucepan or deep, lidded frying pan. Add the mustard seeds and cook until they begin to turn grey and the spluttering begins to subside. Add the optional split peas and fry until light brown, about ½ to 1 minute, stirring constantly. Add the ginger and chillies, cook for 1 minute, and add the ground coriander, turmeric and paprika. Stir together and add the onions. Sauté, stirring, for 5 minutes, or until beginning to brown. Add potatoes and fry 5 minutes, adding more oil if necessary.

4 Add 4 cups hot water and sea salt to taste, and bring to a simmer. Simmer, covered, over low heat for 15 minutes, or until the potatoes are tender.

5 Remove 1½ cups of the mixture and purée in a blender or food processor, or put through a food mill. Return to the pot and mix together well. Adjust salt. Heat through, stirring (a layer might stick to the bottom of the pot but don't let this worry you).

6 Stir in the lemon juice and coriander and serve at once, in bowls.

Vegetable Fritters

Serves 6 to 10.

These are a spicy version of tempura. You can use just one vegetable, such as onions for onion fritters, or cauliflower, or a combination such as broccoli, courgettes (zucchini), carrots, onions and cauliflower.

Imperial (Metric)	American
For the Batter	For the Batter
3 oz (85g) wholemeal pastry or unbleached white flour (Don't use a coarse flour or the batter will be too heavy.)	¾ cup whole wheat pastry or unbleached white flour (Don't use a coarse flour or the batter will be too heavy.)
1 oz (30g) chick pea flour (Use 4 oz (155g) wholemeal pastry or unbleached white in all if chick pea flour is unavailable.)	¼ cup chick pea flour (Use 1 cup whole wheat pastry or unbleached white in all if chick pea flour is unavailable.)
2 teaspoons ground or crushed coriander seeds	2 teaspoons ground or crushed coriander seeds
Pinch of cayenne	Pinch of cayenne
¼ teaspoon ground cumin	¼ teaspoon ground cumin
¾ teaspoon sea salt	¾ teaspoon sea salt
2 tablespoons safflower, sesame or vegetable oil	2 tablespoons safflower, sesame or vegetable oil
2 eggs, separated	2 eggs, separated
8 fl oz (225ml) water	1 cup water
For Onion Fritters	For Onion Fritters
2 lb (1 kilo) onions, sliced in rings	2 pounds onions, sliced in rings
2 oz (55g) unbleached white flour	½ cup unbleached white flour
For Cauliflower Fritters	For Cauliflower Fritters
1 large head cauliflower, broken into florets	1 large head cauliflower, broken into florets
2 oz (55g) unbleached white flour	½ cup unbleached white flour

For Mixed Vegetable Fritters	For Mixed Vegetable Fritters
½ **head broccoli, broken into florets**	½ **head broccoli, broken into florets**
½ **small head cauliflower, broken into florets**	½ **small head cauliflower, broken into florets**
1 onion, sliced in rings	**1 onion, sliced in rings**
1 to 2 courgettes, sliced	**1 to 2 zucchini, sliced**
1 to 2 carrots, sliced or grated	**1 to 2 carrots, sliced or grated**
2 oz (55g) unbleached white flour	½ **cup unbleached white flour**
Oil for deep-frying	**Oil for deep-frying**

First make the batter. Combine the flours, salt, spices, oil, egg yolks and water. Stir together but don't beat. Let stand for 20 minutes. Then beat the egg whites until fluffy and fold them into the batter.

Blanch the broccoli and cauliflower and drain well.

Toss the vegetables in a bowl with the additional flour. If the carrots are grated, taken them up in clumps and dip them in the flour. You will then dip them in the batter to deep-fry them in clumps.

Heat the oil in a wok or deep-fryer to 370 degrees F (185°C). When it is hot, dip the vegetables into the batter, roll them around to coat evenly, and deep-fry a few at a time. They should float to the top and turn a golden brown very quickly. Remove them from the oil with a slotted spoon, allowing excess oil to drip back into the pan, and drain on paper towels. Make sure to let the oil come back up to 370 degrees F between batches.

Keep the fritters warm in a low oven. Serve when all are done with soya (soy) sauce.

Note: This can be held for an hour or so. Just before serving, heat the oil again, drop in for a few seconds to crisp, drain and serve.

Braised Vegetables in Cardamom Nut Sauce

Serves 4 to 6.

Imperial (Metric)	American
½ lb (250g) potatoes, peeled and diced	½ pound potatoes, peeled and diced
½ lb (250g) turnips, peeled and diced	½ pound turnips, peeled and diced
1 carrot, peeled and diced	1 carrot, peeled and diced
2 tablespoons safflower, sunflower or light vegetable oil	2 tablespoons safflower, or light vegetable oil
2 medium-sized onions, finely chopped	2 medium-sized, onions, finely chopped
2 large cloves garlic, minced	2 large cloves garlic, minced
1 tablespoon minced fresh ginger	1 tablespoon minced fresh ginger
1 green chilli, seeded and minced	1 green chili, seeded and minced
12 green or 9 white cardamom pods	12 green or 9 white cardamom pods
1 stick cinnamon, 3 inches (6cm) long	1 stick cinnamon, 3 inches long
24 whole cloves	24 whole cloves
5 tablespoons ground, blanched almonds	5 tablespoons ground, blanched almonds
8 fl oz (225ml) natural low-fat yogurt	1 cup plain low-fat yogurt
6 oz (170g) shelled fresh green or frozen peas, defrosted	1 cup shelled fresh green or frozen peas, defrosted
Salt to taste	Salt to taste
2 fl oz (60ml) double cream	¼ cup heavy cream

1   Place the diced potatoes, turnips and carrots in a bowl of cold water while you work with the remaining ingredients.

 Have the spices measured out and ready, right next to the stove. Heat the oil in a large, heavy-bottomed, lidded frying pan or casserole and add the onions, garlic, ginger and chilli pepper. Sauté, stirring constantly, over medium heat until the onions begin to turn light brown, about 10 minutes. Add the cardamom, cinnamon and cloves and continue to stir-fry another 5 minutes (add a little more oil if necessary). Add the ground almonds and stir together well.

 Add 2 tablespoons of the yogurt and stir-fry the mixture until the yogurt evaporates. Continue adding yogurt in 2-tablespoon amounts until the cup is used up, stirring constantly to avoid sticking.

 Drain the carrots, turnips and potatoes and add to the pot along with 12 fl oz (340ml/1½ cups) hot water. If using fresh peas, add them now. Add salt to taste, cover and reduce heat to medium-low. Cook, stirring occasionally, for about 30 minutes, or until the vegetables are tender. Add the cream and frozen peas, stir together and cook uncovered for 10 minutes. If after 10 minutes the sauce is not very thick, increase heat to medium and simmer until it reaches the desired consistency. If it is too thick, thin out with a little hot water or milk. Correct salt and serve over hot cooked grains.

Note: This tastes best if prepared a day ahead and will keep in the refrigerator for up to 4 days.

Tzimmes

Serves 6.

Tzimmes (pronounced 'tsimmis') is a traditional Jewish sweet potato casserole. It is served at Jewish holiday dinners but needn't be reserved for just these days.

Imperial (Metric)	American
3 large sweet potatoes, well scrubbed	**3 large sweet potatoes, well scrubbed**
8 fl oz (225ml) natural low-fat yogurt	**1 cup plain low-fat yogurt**
3 tablespoons butter	**3 tablespoons butter**
½ lb (250g) carrots, peeled and grated	**½ pound carrots, peeled and grated**
½ lb (250g) tart apples, peeled, cored and grated	**½ pound tart apples, peeled, cored and grated**
2 tablespoons mild-flavoured honey	**2 tablespoons mild-flavored honey**
4 oz (115g) raisins	**⅔ cup raisins**
2½ oz (70g) chopped walnuts or pecans	**½ cup chopped walnuts or pecans**
½ teaspoon cinnamon	**½ teaspoon cinnamon**
¼ teaspoon ground cloves	**¼ teaspoon ground cloves**
¼ teaspoon ground nutmeg	**¼ teaspoon ground nutmeg**
¼ teaspoon sea salt	**¼ teaspoon sea salt**

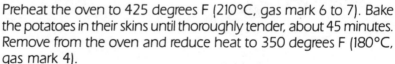

1 Preheat the oven to 425 degrees F (210°C, gas mark 6 to 7). Bake the potatoes in their skins until thoroughly tender, about 45 minutes. Remove from the oven and reduce heat to 350 degrees F (180°C, gas mark 4).

2 Scoop out the potato from the peel, discard the peels and purée the potatoes in a food processor fitted with the steel blade, or through a food mill. Mix in the yogurt and 1 tablespoon of butter. Set aside.

3 Heat the remaining butter in a heavy-bottomed casserole or frying pan and add the carrots. Sauté, stirring, for about 5 minutes, then stir in the apples and sauté another 5 minutes. Remove from the heat and add the honey, raisins, nuts, spices and sea salt. Stir in the sweet potato purée and mix everything together well.

4 Transfer to an oiled or buttered baking dish or casserole, cover with foil or a lid and bake in the preheated oven for 20 to 30 minutes. Serve hot.

Celery au Cumin

Serves 4.

Imperial (Metric)	American
1 lb (500g) celery, washed and sliced	1 pound celery, washed and sliced
Juice of 2 lemons	Juice of 2 lemons
2 fl oz (60ml) olive oil	¼ cup olive oil
¾ teaspoon ground cumin	¾ teaspoon ground cumin
Pinch of sea salt	Pinch of sea salt
Freshly ground pepper, to taste	Freshly ground pepper, to taste
Minced fresh parsley, for garnish	Minced fresh parsley, for garnish

1 Heat the lemon juice and olive oil in a heavy-bottomed lidded casserole. Add the remaining ingredients, stir together well, cover and simmer over low heat for 20 to 30 minutes.

2 Remove from the heat, transfer to a bowl and chill several hours. Sprinkle with parsley and serve.

Curried Pumpkin-Sweet Potato Purée

Serves 6 to 8.

Imperial (Metric)	American
2 lb (1 kilo) fresh pumpkin, peeled, seeded and diced	2 pounds fresh pumpkin or winter squash, peeled, seeded and diced
½ lb (250g) sweet potato, baked in its skin until tender	½ pound sweet potato, baked in its skin until tender
2 tablespoons lime juice	2 tablespoons lime juice
3 tablespoons natural low-fat yogurt, more if needed	3 tablespoons plain low-fat yogurt, more if needed
2 tablespoons melted butter	2 tablespoons melted butter
1 teaspoon minced or grated fresh ginger, or ¼ teaspoon ground dried	1 teaspoon minced or grated fresh ginger, or ¼ teaspoon ground dried
2 teaspoons curry powder	2 teaspoons curry powder
¼ teaspoon cinnamon	¼ teaspoon cinnamon
Pinch of nutmeg	Pinch of nutmeg
Sea salt and freshly ground pepper to taste	Sea salt and freshly ground pepper to taste

1   Steam the pumpkin for 15 minutes, or until thoroughly tender. Drain and let drip for a few minutes in a colander.

2   Remove the skin from the baked sweet potato, and purée with the pumpkin in a food processor or through a food mill. Stir in the yogurt and lime juice and combine well.

3   Melt the butter in a large, heavy-bottomed frying pan or casserole over low heat and add the ginger and curry powder. Cook gently, stirring, for 1 to 2 minutes. Stir in the pumpkin-sweet potato purée, the cinnamon, nutmeg, sea salt and freshly ground pepper and heat through, stirring. Transfer to a serving dish and serve, or keep warm in a medium oven.

Steamed Peas with Mild Yogurt Sauce

Serves 4.

Imperial (Metric)	American
1½ lb (750g) fresh peas, shelled	1½ pounds fresh peas, shelled
8 fl oz (225ml) natural low-fat yogurt	1 cup plain, low-fat yogurt
1 teaspoon ground cumin	1 teaspoon ground cumin
½ teaspoon ground coriander	½ teaspoon ground coriander
Sea salt to taste	Sea salt to taste
2 teaspoons lemon juice	2 teaspoons lemon juice

1 Steam the peas until tender, about 10 to 15 minutes.

2 Meanwhile mix together the yogurt, spices and sea salt to taste. Stir in the lemon juice.

3 When the peas are done, drain and toss at once with the sauce. Serve.

Peas with Ginger, Spices and Fresh Coriander

Serves 6.

Imperial (Metric)	American
2½ lb (1.25 kilos) fresh peas, shelled	2½ pounds fresh peas, shelled
2 tablespoons safflower or peanut oil	2 tablespoons safflower or peanut oil
¼ teaspoon whole black mustard seeds	¼ teaspoon whole black mustard seeds
5 whole fenugreek seeds	5 whole fenugreek seeds
1 piece fresh ginger, about 2 inches (5cm) long, peeled and finely minced or grated	1 piece fresh ginger, about 2 inches long, peeled and finely minced or grated
¼ teaspoon ground turmeric	¼ teaspoon ground turmeric
1 teaspoon ground coriander	1 teaspoon ground coriander
1 teaspoon ground cumin	1 teaspoon ground cumin
1 teaspoon Garam Masala (see page 26)	1 teaspoon Garam Masala (see page 26)
Sea salt to taste	Sea salt to taste
4 tablespoons water or white wine	4 tablespoons water or white wine
½ oz (15g) chopped fresh coriander	½ cup chopped fresh coriander

1 Steam the peas for 5 minutes and refresh under cold water.

2 Heat the safflower or peanut oil over medium heat in a large, heavy-bottomed frying pan or wok and sauté the mustard seeds and fenugreek seeds for about 10 seconds. Add the ginger and turmeric and stir-fry about 2 minutes, being careful not to allow the ginger to burn (reduce heat if oil is too hot). Add the remaining spices and the sea salt, stir together, then stir in 4 tablespoons water or white wine and mix together well. Add the peas, toss together for a minute or so and reduce heat, cover and simmer 15 minutes, or until the peas are tender, checking the liquid every 5 minutes. Add more if necessary.

3 When the peas are tender, stir in the chopped fresh coriander and serve.

Spicy Sautéed Courgettes (Zucchini) and Tomatoes

Serves 4 to 6.

Imperial (Metric)	American
1 tablespoon safflower or vegetable oil	1 tablespoon safflower or vegetable oil
1 small onion, chopped	1 small onion, chopped
2 cloves garlic, minced or put through a press	2 cloves garlic, minced or put through a press
2 serrano or jalapeño peppers, seeded and minced	2 serrano or jalapeño peppers, seeded and minced
½ teaspoon ground cumin	½ teaspoon ground cumin
¼ teaspoon chilli powder	¼ teaspoon chili powder
1½ lb (750g) courgettes, diced	1½ pounds zucchini, diced
1 lb (500g) tomatoes, seeded and diced	1 pound tomatoes, seeded and diced
2 tablespoons lemon juice	2 tablespoons lemon juice
Sea salt and freshly ground pepper to taste	Sea salt and freshly ground pepper to taste
2 tablespoons chopped fresh coriander	2 tablespoons chopped fresh coriander

1 Heat the oil in a large, heavy-bottomed frying pan or casserole and add the onion and garlic. Sauté until the onion begins to soften and add the minced peppers, the spices, the courgettes (zucchini) and the tomatoes. Sauté, stirring, for a couple of minutes (add more oil if necessary), then cover and cook over medium-low heat for 10 to 15 minutes, stirring occasionally.

2 Season to taste with lemon juice, sea salt and freshly ground pepper. Stir in the coriander and serve.

Louisiana-Style Courgettes (Summer Squash)

This spicy, fried dish is a toned-down version of Chef Paul Prudhomme's, from his *Louisiana Kitchen* (William Morrow & Co., 1984).

Imperial (Metric)	American
½ teaspoon sea salt	½ teaspoon sea salt
¾ teaspoon sweet paprika	¾ teaspoon sweet paprika
½ teaspoon ground white pepper	½ teaspoon ground white pepper
¼ to ½ teaspoon cayenne pepper, to taste	¼ to ½ teaspoon cayenne pepper, to taste
½ teaspoon ground black pepper	½ teaspoon ground black pepper
¼ teaspoon dried thyme leaves	¼ teaspoon dried thyme leaves
1½ lb (750g) courgettes, cut in rounds	1½ pounds zucchini or summer squash, cut in rounds
2 oz (55g) wholemeal pastry flour	½ cup whole wheat pastry flour
2 oz (55g) cornmeal	½ cup cornmeal
4 fl oz (120ml) cup milk	½ cup milk
1 egg	1 egg
Safflower or peanut oil for deep-frying	Safflower or peanut oil for deep-frying

1 Combine the sea salt, spices and thyme in a small bowl. Sprinkle the diced courgettes (squash) with a teaspoon of the mix.

2 Divide the remaining spice mix in half and stir one half into the flour and the other half into the cornmeal.

3 Beat together the egg and milk.

4 Heat 1 inch of safflower or peanut oil in a deep saucepan or frying pan to 350 degrees F (180°C).

5 Using your hands, quickly toss the courgettes (squash) in the flour and shake off any excess flour. Toss in the milk and egg, then dip in the cornmeal to coat. Shake off any excess cornmeal and deep-fry for about 2 minutes. Drain on paper towels and serve at once.

Spicy Okra and Tomato Sauté

Serves 4 to 6.

Imperial (Metric)	American
1 tablespoon safflower or vegetable oil	1 tablespoon safflower or vegetable oil
1 large onion, chopped	1 large onion, chopped
2 cloves garlic, minced or put through a press	2 cloves garlic, minced or put through a press
2 teaspoons sweet paprika	2 teaspoons sweet paprika
1 hot green chilli pepper, chopped	1 hot green chilli pepper, chopped
1 lb (500g) okra, trimmed just below the stem (before the seeds begin) and sliced ¼ to ½ inch (5mm-1cm) thick	1 pound okra, trimmed just below the stem (before the seeds begin) and sliced ¼ to ½ inch thick
1 tablespoon wine vinegar	1 tablespoon wine vinegar
3 tablespoons white wine	3 tablespoons white wine
1 lb (500g) tomatoes, fresh or canned, sliced	1 pound tomatoes, fresh or canned, sliced
1 tablespoon chopped fresh basil or coriander	1 tablespoon chopped fresh basil or coriander
Sea salt and freshly ground pepper to taste	Sea salt and freshly ground pepper to taste

1 Heat the oil in a large, heavy-bottomed frying pan or casserole and add the onion and 1 clove of the garlic. Sauté over medium heat until the onion begins to soften. Add the paprika and chilli pepper and continue to sauté another few minutes, stirring.

2 Add the okra and vinegar and sauté until the okra turns bright green, about 5 minutes. Add the wine, tomatoes and remaining garlic and cook, stirring from time to time, for 10 to 15 minutes, or until the okra is tender and the mixture aromatic. Add the basil or coriander and season to taste with sea salt and freshly ground pepper. Serve with hot, cooked grains.

Gingered Mushrooms

Serves 4 to 6.

Imperial (Metric)	American
1 tablespoon safflower or vegetable oil	1 tablespoon safflower or vegetable oil
1½ lb (750g) mushrooms, cleaned, stems trimmed, cut in halves or quarters if very large	1½ pounds mushrooms, cleaned, stems trimmed, cut in halves or quarters if very large
2 shallots, finely chopped	2 shallots, finely chopped
2 cloves garlic, minced or put through a press	2 cloves garlic, minced or put through a press
2 teaspoons minced or grated fresh ginger	2 teaspoons minced or grated fresh ginger
Pinch of cayenne	Pinch of cayenne
1 tablespoon soya sauce	1 tablespoon soy sauce
2 tablespoons dry white wine	2 tablespoons dry white wine
¼ teaspoon thyme	¼ teaspoon thyme
Freshly ground pepper to taste	Freshly ground pepper to taste

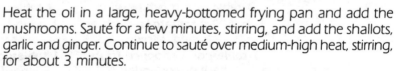 Heat the oil in a large, heavy-bottomed frying pan and add the mushrooms. Sauté for a few minutes, stirring, and add the shallots, garlic and ginger. Continue to sauté over medium-high heat, stirring, for about 3 minutes.

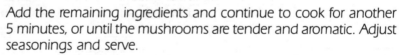 Add the remaining ingredients and continue to cook for another 5 minutes, or until the mushrooms are tender and aromatic. Adjust seasonings and serve.

Cucumbers Simmered in White Wine

Serves 4 to 6.

Imperial (Metric)	American
1 tablespoon olive or safflower oil	1 tablespoon olive or safflower oil
1 onion, thinly sliced	1 onion, thinly sliced
1 teaspoon ground cumin	1 teaspoon ground cumin
1 teaspoon curry powder	1 teaspoon curry powder
2 large or 4 small cucumbers, peeled and sliced	2 large or 4 small cucumbers, peeled and sliced
Pinch of cayenne	Pinch of cayenne
Juice of ½ lemon	Juice of ½ lemon
8 fl oz (225ml) dry white wine	1 cup dry white wine
Sea salt and freshly ground pepper to taste	Sea salt and freshly ground pepper to taste
2 tablespoons chopped fresh parsley or coriander	2 tablespoons chopped fresh parsley or coriander

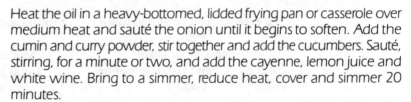

1 Heat the oil in a heavy-bottomed, lidded frying pan or casserole over medium heat and sauté the onion until it begins to soften. Add the cumin and curry powder, stir together and add the cucumbers. Sauté, stirring, for a minute or two, and add the cayenne, lemon juice and white wine. Bring to a simmer, reduce heat, cover and simmer 20 minutes.

2 Uncover and turn up the heat. Boil off most of the wine, stirring. Add sea salt and freshly ground pepper to taste, toss with the parsley or fresh coriander and serve, or chill and serve cold.

Sweet and Sour Red Cabbage with Apples

Serves 4.

Imperial (Metric)	American
1 to 2 tablespoons safflower or vegetable oil	1 to 2 tablespoons safflower or vegetable oil
1 onion, sliced	1 onion, sliced
1 lb (500g) red cabbage, cored and shredded	1 pound red cabbage, cored and shredded
2 tart apples, peeled, cored and sliced	2 tart apples, peeled, cored and sliced
3 tablespoons apple cider or red wine vinegar	3 tablespoons apple cider or red wine vinegar
2 tablespoons raisins	2 tablespoons raisins
½ teaspoon ground cloves	½ teaspoon ground cloves
½ teaspoon ground allspice	½ teaspoon ground allspice
1 teaspoon ground cinnamon	1 teaspoon ground cinnamon
2 fl oz (60ml) beer or apple juice	¼ cup beer or apple juice
2 tablespoons mild-flavoured honey	2 tablespoons mild-flavored honey
Sea salt to taste	Sea salt to taste
8 fl oz (225ml) natural low-fat yogurt	1 cup plain low-fat yogurt

Heat 1 tablespoon of the oil in a large, heavy-bottomed frying pan and add the onion. Sauté, stirring, over medium heat until the onion begins to brown, and add the cabbage. Sauté a few minutes (add more oil if necessary) and add the apples, vinegar, raisins and spices and stir together well. Add the beer or apple juice and the honey and continue to cook, stirring occasionally, for 10 to 15 minutes. Season to taste with sea salt and freshly ground pepper and remove from the heat. Let cool a moment and stir in the yogurt. Serve at once over hot cooked grains such as bulgur or kasha.

Vegetables en Papillote with Garam Masala

Serves 4 to 6.

Imperial (Metric)	American
1 lb (500g) new potatoes, cut in half or quarters	1 pound new potatoes, cut in half or quarters
1 bulb fennel, sliced	1 bulb fennel, sliced
1 head garlic, broken into cloves, peeled	1 head garlic, broken into cloves, peeled
8 whole shallots, peeled	8 whole shallots, peeled
1½ tablespoons vegetable oil	1½ tablespoons vegetable oil
Sea salt and freshly ground pepper to taste	Sea salt and freshly ground pepper to taste
1½ teaspoons Garam Masala (page 26)	1½ teaspoons Garam Masala (page 26)

1   Prepare a grill or preheat the oven to 375 degrees F (190°C, gas mark 5).

2   Cut 4 to 6 double-thickness squares of aluminum foil, about 12 inches (25cm) square, and brush with vegetable oil.

3   Toss together the prepared vegetables with the remaining oil, sea salt and freshly ground pepper, and the garam masala. Distribute evenly among the squares of foil.

4   Bring the edges of the foil up around the vegetables and crimp together tightly. Place directly on the coals of the grill or in the preheated oven and bake 45 minutes. Serve directly from the foil.

Gingered Carrots

Serves 4 to 6.

Imperial (Metric)	American
1½ lb (750g) carrots, peeled and thinly sliced	1½ pounds carrots, peeled and thinly sliced
1 tablespoon butter	1 tablespoon butter
6 tablespoons fresh orange juice	⅓ cup fresh orange juice
2 tablespoons mild-flavoured honey	2 tablespoons mild-flavored honey
1 tablespoon grated orange rind	1 tablespoon grated orange rind
1 teaspoon grated or minced fresh ginger	1 teaspoon grated or minced fresh ginger
¼ teaspoon ground cloves	¼ teaspoon ground cloves
3 tablespoons red wine	3 tablespoons red wine

1 Heat the butter in a heavy-bottomed saucepan or casserole. Add the carrots and ginger and sauté for 2 minutes over medium heat.

2 Add the remaining ingredients and bring to a simmer. Cover and simmer 10 minutes.

3 Remove the lid and turn up the heat. Reduce the liquid until it glazes the carrots. Correct seasonings and serve.

Spicy Green Beans

Serves 4 to 6.

Imperial (Metric)	American
1½ lb (750g) green beans, ends trimmed	1½ pounds green beans, ends trimmed
3 tablespoons natural low-fat yogurt	3 tablespoons plain low-fat yogurt
1 teaspoon mild-flavoured honey	1 teaspoon mild-flavored honey
½ hot fresh green chilli, thinly sliced	½ hot, fresh, green chilli, thinly sliced
1 teaspoon cornflour	1 teaspoon cornstarch
Sea salt to taste	Sea salt to taste
¾ teaspoon dry English mustard	¾ teaspoon dry English mustard
¾ teaspoon ground cumin	¾ teaspoon ground cumin
1 tablespoon lemon juice	1 tablespoon lemon juice
3 tablespoons safflower or peanut oil	3 tablespoons safflower or peanut oil
5 whole fenugreek seeds	5 whole fenugreek seeds
¼ teaspoon whole cumin	¼ teaspooon whole cumin
¼ teaspoon Garam Masala (see page 26)	¼ teaspoon Garam Masala (see page 26)
3 tablespoons chopped fresh coriander	3 tablespoons chopped fresh coriander

 Steam the beans for 10 minutes. Drain, refresh under cold water and slice into thin rounds about ¼ inch thick. Set aside.

 In a small bowl combine the yogurt, green chilli, sea salt, honey, dry mustard, cornflour (starch), ground cumin and lemon juice. Add 3 tablespoons water and mix well.

 Heat the oil in a wide, heavy-bottomed frying pan or wok over medium-high heat. Add the fenugreek and cumin seeds and the garam masala, stir-fry 20 seconds and add the beans. Cook, tossing, for a minute, then reduce heat to low. Add the yogurt mixture, stir everything together well, and cover and simmer 15 minutes over low heat, stirring from time to time. Stir in the chopped fresh coriander, correct seasonings and serve with hot, cooked grains.

4. Tofu, Grains, Legumes and Pastas

Tofu Quiche

Serves 6 to 8.

Imperial (Metric)	American
For the Mixed Grains Pastry Base	For the Mixed Grains Pie Crust
2 oz (55g) millet meal, made by blending millet in a blender at high speed	½ cup millet meal, made by blending millet in a blender at high speed
1 oz (30g) cornmeal	¼ cup cornmeal
3 oz (85g) wholemeal pastry flour	¾ cup whole wheat pastry flour
¼ teaspoon salt	¼ teaspoon salt
4 tablespoons safflower oil	¼ cup safflower oil
2 to 3 tablespoons cold water	2 to 3 tablespoons cold water
More oil or water if necessary	More oil or water if necessary

1 Oil a 9- or 10-inch (23-25cm) pie pan or quiche pan. Preheat the oven to 350 degrees F (180°C, gas mark 4)

2 Mix together the millet meal and cornmeal and toast in a dry skillet over medium heat until just beginning to smell toasty. Immediately remove from the heat and place in a mixing bowl. Add the pastry flour and salt, and cut in the oil with a fork or pastry cutter. Add the water and mix thoroughly.

3 This pastry (crust) won't gather neatly into a ball the way other pastries (crusts) do, and must be pressed into the pie pan or quiche pan.

Pick it up in little pieces and press them piece by piece into the pan, or gather up the mass and press, pressing from the ball of your palm out to your fingertips. When the pastry bakes it firms up, so don't worry about the crumbly quality.

4 Prebake the pastry 5 minutes in the oven.

For the Quiche	For the Quiche
1 tablespoon safflower or vegetable oil	1 tablespoon safflower or vegetable oil
1 medium-sized onion, finely chopped	1 medium-sized onion, finely chopped
1 to 2 cloves garlic, minced or put through a press	1 to 2 cloves garlic, minced or put through a press
1 teaspoon minced fresh ginger	1 teaspoon minced fresh ginger
1½ teaspoons curry powder	1½ teaspoons curry powder
1½ lb (750g) tofu	1½ pounds tofu
2 eggs	2 eggs
4 fl oz (120ml) natural low-fat yogurt	½ cup plain low-fat yogurt
⅛ teaspoon cayenne	⅛ teaspoon cayenne
1 additional tablespoon safflower or sesame oil	1 additional tablespoon safflower or sesame oil
⅛ teaspoon freshly ground nutmeg	⅛ teaspoon freshly ground nutmeg
2 to 3 tablespoons tamari soya sauce, to taste	2 to 3 tablespoons tamari soy sauce, to taste
1 teaspoon lemon juice	1 teaspoon lemon juice
2 tablespoons sesame tahini	2 tablespoons sesame tahini
1 to 2 tablespoons dry sherry, to taste	1 to 2 tablespoons dry sherry, to taste
Freshly ground pepper to taste	Freshly ground pepper, to taste

Optional	Optional
10 oz (285g) spinach, washed, stemmed, blanched, squeezed dry and chopped OR 12 oz (340g) broccoli florets, steamed 5 minutes and coarsely chopped OR 4 oz (115g) mushrooms, sliced and sautéed until tender in 1 tablespoon safflower or vegetable oil	10 ounces spinach, washed, stemmed, blanched, squeezed dry and chopped OR 2 cups broccoli florets, steamed 5 minutes and coarsely chopped OR 2 cups mushrooms, sliced and sautéed until tender in 1 tablespoon safflower or vegetable oil

Continued over page

1 Preheat the oven to 350 degrees F (180°C, gas mark 4).

2 Heat the first tablespoon of oil in a heavy-bottomed frying pan and sauté the onion over medium-low heat with the garlic, minced ginger and 1 teaspoon of the curry powder until the onion is tender and translucent. Set aside (if using mushrooms, sauté with the onion until tender).

3 Blend all the remaining ingredients (except the optional spinach or broccoli) together in a blender or food processor until completely smooth. Stir in the onion mixture and the optionals. Adjust seasonings, adding more soya (soy) sauce, pepper or curry powder if you wish.

4 Pour the tofu mixture into the prebaked pastry case (pie crust). Bake at 350 degrees F (180°C, gas mark 4) for 30 minutes, or until the top begins to brown. Let sit about 10 minutes before serving.

Note: You can also make this quiche without the pastry or bake it in an oiled paté tureen or bread pan and use as a spread.

Aubergine (Eggplant) Moussaka with Tofu Bechamel

Serves 8 to 10.

Imperial (Metric)	American
For the Moussaka	**For the Moussaka**
3 large aubergines	**3 large eggplants**
1 tablespoon olive oil	**1 tablespoon olive oil**
2 additional tablespoons olive oil, safflower oil or butter	**2 additional tablespoons olive oil, safflower oil or butter**
1 large onion, chopped	**1 large onion, chopped**
3 cloves garlic, minced or put through a press	**3 cloves garlic, minced or put through a press**
2½ oz (70g) sliced fresh mushrooms	**1 cup sliced fresh mushrooms**
1 bell pepper, cored, seeded and diced	**1 bell pepper, cored, seeded and diced**
3 tomatoes, peeled, seeded and chopped	**3 tomatoes, peeled, seeded and chopped**
4 fl oz (120ml) dry white wine	**½ cup dry white wine**
½ to 1 teaspoon thyme, to taste	**½ to 1 teaspoon thyme, to taste**
1 teaspoon oregano, or more to taste	**1 teaspoon oregano, or more to taste**
3 oz (85g) raw soya grits, cooked,* or bulgur, cooked*	**½ cup raw soy grits, cooked,* or bulgur, cooked***
½ teaspoon cinnamon	**½ teaspoon cinnamon**
½ teaspoon allspice, or more, to taste	**½ teaspoon allspice, or more, to taste**
½ oz (15g) chopped, fresh parsley	**½ cup chopped, fresh parsley**
Sea salt and freshly ground pepper to taste	**Sea salt and freshly ground pepper to taste**
4 oz (115g) freshly grated Parmesan	**1 cup freshly grated Parmesan**

Continued over page

*To cook the soya (soy) grits, combine with ¾ pints (425ml/2 cups) water in a heavy saucepan and bring to a boil. Reduce the heat and simmer, covered, for 50 minutes. Add sea salt to taste and drain off excess water.

To cook the bulgur, place in a bowl and pour on 8 fl oz (225ml/1 cup) of boiling water. Let sit 20 to 30 minutes, until fluffy. Drain off excess water. Add sea salt to taste.

For the Tofu Bechamel	For the Tofu Bechamel
1 lb (500g) tofu	1 pound tofu
1 tablespoon dark soya sauce such as tamari or Kikkoman	1 tablespoon dark soy sauce such as tamari or Kikkoman
1½ tablespoons miso paste (a fermented soya paste available in Japanese and wholefood stores), or one additional tablespoon soya sauce	1½ tablespoons miso paste (a fermented soy paste available in Japanese and whole food stores), or one additional tablespoon soy sauce
4 fl oz (120ml) natural low-fat yogurt	½ cup plain low-fat yogurt
2 fl oz (60ml) water	¼ cup water
1 teaspoon minced fresh ginger	1 teaspoon minced fresh ginger
3 tablespoons sesame tahini	3 tablespoons sesame tahini
3 tablespoons dry sherry	3 tablespoons dry sherry
1 tablespoon lemon juice	1 tablespoon lemon juice
Pinch of freshly grated nutmeg	Pinch of freshly grated nutmeg
Small pinch of cayenne	Small pinch of cayenne

1 Preheat the oven to 450 degrees F (220°C, gas mark 7). Oil a large baking sheet with olive oil.

2 Slice the aubergines (eggplants) in half lengthwise and score with a sharp knife, being careful not to cut through the skin. Place cut side down on the baking sheet and bake 15 to 20 minutes in the preheated oven, or until the skins begin to shrivel. Meanwhile prepare the remaining ingredients. Remove the aubergines (eggplants) from the oven, and when cool enough to handle scoop out the pulp and dice. Reduce the oven heat to 350 degrees F (180°C, gas mark 4).

3 Heat a large, heavy-bottomed frying pan or wok. Add the additional olive oil, safflower oil or butter and sauté the onion with the garlic until the onion is tender. Add the mushrooms, bell pepper and tomatoes and sauté 3 minutes, stirring. Add the wine, thyme, oregano and the diced eggplant and toss together (aubergine/eggplant will be very soft). Cover and simmer over medium heat for 15 minutes, stirring from time to time. Uncover and stir in the cooked soya (soy) grits or bulgur, the cinnamon, allspice, parsley, sea salt and pepper to taste, and cook, stirring another 2 minutes. Taste and adjust seasonings, and remove from the heat.

4 Place all the ingredients for the tofu bechamel in a blender or food processor and blend at high speed until completely smooth. Make sure you leave no gritty chunks.

5 Spread half the aubergine (eggplant) mixture over the bottom of an oiled 11 × 16 inch (22 × 32cm) baking dish or a 6-7 pint (3 litres/4- to 5-quart) casserole. Sprinkle ⅓ of the Parmesan over this. Spread the remaining eggplant mixture over this and sprinkle on another ⅓ cup of the Parmesan. Mix the remaining Parmesan into the tofu bechamel and spread the sauce in a thick layer over the top of the casserole.

6 Bake in the preheated oven for 25 to 30 minutes, or until the top browns.

Tempura'd Tofu

Serves 4 to 6.

Imperial (Metric)	American
For the Tofu	For the Tofu
1½ lb (750g) pressed tofu*	1½ pounds pressed tofu*
4 fl oz (120ml) dark soya sauce such as tamari or Kikkoman	½ cup dark soy sauce such as tamari or Kikkoman
2 fl oz (60ml) water	¼ cup water
1 clove garlic, crushed	1 clove garlic, crushed
1 teaspoon minced fresh ginger	1 teaspoon minced fresh ginger
½ teaspoon cinnamon	½ teaspoon cinnamon
¼ teaspoon ground allspice	¼ teaspoon ground allspice
¼ teaspoon crushed anise or fennel seeds	¼ teaspoon crushed anise or fennel seeds
⅛ teaspoon ground cloves	⅛ teaspoon ground cloves
1 to 2 oz (30 to 55g) wholemeal pastry flour, as needed	¼ to ½ cup whole wheat pastry flour, as needed
1½ pints (1 litre) safflower or vegetable oil, for deep-frying	1 quart safflower or vegetable oil, for deep-frying
For the Batter	For the Batter
½ teaspoon sea salt	½ teaspoon sea salt
4 oz (115g) sifted wholemeal pastry flour, or a combination of wholemeal pastry and unbleached white flour	1 cup sifted whole wheat pastry flour, or a combination of whole wheat pastry and unbleached white flour
2 tablespoons safflower, sesame or vegetable oil	2 tablespoons safflower, sesame or vegetable oil
2 eggs, separated	2 eggs, separated
8 fl oz (225ml) water	1 cup water

To Press Tofu for Tempuras and Stir-Fries: Cut tofu into 4-ounce (115g) squares and wrap in a dish cloth. Place two layers of paper towel on a baking sheet and set the tofu on top. Set a cutting board or another baking sheet on top of the tofu, and weight that with a

4-5 pint (3-4 litres/3-4-quart) saucepan filled with water, or a heavy casserole. Press for an hour. Refrigerate wrapped in a wet towel, if not using right away. Pressed tofu stays together better than unpressed tofu when you cook it, and has an almost chicken-like texture.

1 Make the batter. Combine the flour, salt, oil, egg yolks and water. Stir together but don't beat. Let stand for 20 minutes while you simmer the tofu (see Step 2). Then whip the egg whites until fluffy but not stiff, and fold them into the batter.

2 While the batter is resting, combine the soya (soy) sauce, water, garlic, ginger and spices in a saucepan and bring to a simmer. Cut the pressed tofu into slivers ¼ to ½ inch (5mm-1cm) wide and simmer in the soya (soy) sauce mixture for 15 minutes. Remove with a slotted spoon and drain. Retain the soya (soy) sauce for dipping.

3 Slowly heat the oil in a saucepan, wok or deep-fryer to 370 degrees F (190°C). It is important to get the oil to this temperature before attempting to deep-fry, and to maintain the temperature throughout.

4 Carefully dredge the tofu in the flour, then dip into the batter. Deep-fry until golden brown and drain on paper towels. Arrange on a platter with other vegetables, garnish with parsley or fresh coriander and serve with the simmering liquid.

Stuffed Tofu Pockets, Squares or Triangles

Serves 4.

This is one of the most convenient and intriguing ways to serve bean curd. You press 12-ounce (340g) squares, cut them into two large triangles or squares, then deep-fry the pressed tofu. This gives it a tough outer skin and renders it almost like chicken. Then you scoop out the insides and stuff the hollowed out shell, as if it were pitta bread. Or you can leave the tofu in the shape of squares and scoop out the middle so that it's like a box. A number of fillings will work. In addition to the delicious suggestions below, the pressed, deep-fried tofu makes a great container for leftovers.

Serving tofu this way increases the protein content of your meal tremendously. A pressed 12-ounce (340g) square is not much more filling than a 4-ounce (115g) piece, the usual serving, but it has three times as much protein.

One thing that's great about these is that they keep for a longer time than fresh, unpressed tofu. Once pressed and deep-fried, they needn't be covered with water; just keep them in the refrigerator in a covered container. They will hold for up to three days this way, and if you have them on hand you can have marvellous stuffed tofu dinners in minutes.

Imperial (Metric)	American
4 12-oz (340g) squares tofu	4 12-ounce squares tofu
1½ pints (1 litre) safflower or vegetable oil, for deep-frying	1 quart safflower or vegetable oil, for deep-frying
Soya sauce, if desired	Soy sauce, if desired

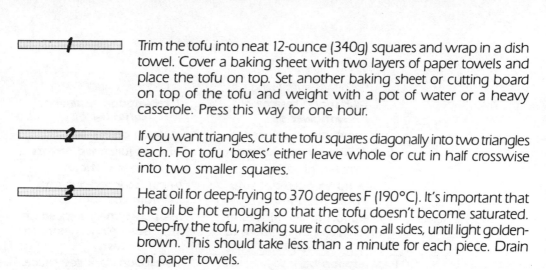

1 Trim the tofu into neat 12-ounce (340g) squares and wrap in a dish towel. Cover a baking sheet with two layers of paper towels and place the tofu on top. Set another baking sheet or cutting board on top of the tofu and weight with a pot of water or a heavy casserole. Press this way for one hour.

2 If you want triangles, cut the tofu squares diagonally into two triangles each. For tofu 'boxes' either leave whole or cut in half crosswise into two smaller squares.

3 Heat oil for deep-frying to 370 degrees F (190°C). It's important that the oil be hot enough so that the tofu doesn't become saturated. Deep-fry the tofu, making sure it cooks on all sides, until light golden-brown. This should take less than a minute for each piece. Drain on paper towels.

4 When the tofu is cool enough to handle, take a sharp knife and, leaving a quarter-inch margin around the edges, carefully scoop out a pocket from the diagonal edge of your triangle. The tofu should be firm from the pressing and deep-frying, and won't be too fragile. Set the scooped-out tofu aside for another use (it could be used as an ingredient in the filling). If you are making stuffed tofu squares, cut out an inside box, leaving a quarter inch margin, and carefully scoop out the tofu. Douse the inside with soya (soy) sauce if you wish.

5 You should be able to get about ¼ cup of filling into the triangles, and more into the squares. Hold the deep-fried tofu in the refrigerator until ready to fill, or hold the filled triangles or squares in the refrigerator until ready to serve. These can be served cold, at room temperature or hot. To serve hot heat through in a 325 degree F (170°C, gas mark 3) oven for 20 minutes.

For variations, see over

Cashew Carrot Filling	Cashew Carrot Filling
1 tablespoon sesame or safflower oil	1 tablespoon sesame or safflower oil
1 small onion, minced	1 small onion, minced
½ lb (250g) carrots, julienned	1½ cups julienned carrots
4 oz (115g) cashews	¾ cup cashews
1 teacup scooped-out tofu from the squares	¾ cup scooped-out tofu from the squares
1 teaspoon finely minced or grated fresh ginger (more to taste)	1 teaspoon finely minced or grated fresh ginger (more to taste)
1 tablespoon dark soya sauce, such as tamari or Kikkoman	1 tablespoon dark soy sauce, such as tamari or Kikkoman
1 small, hot, dried red chilli pepper, minced, or ½ teaspoon hot pepper oil, available in Oriental markets	1 small, hot, dried red chili pepper, minced, or ½ teaspoon hot pepper oil, available in Oriental markets
4 oz (115g) shredded cucumber	½ cup shredded cucumber
1 tablespoon Pernod or anise-flavoured liqueur	1 tablespoon Pernod or anise-flavored liqueur
3 tablespoons chopped fresh coriander	3 tablespoons chopped fresh coriander

Heat the oil in a wok or heavy-bottomed frying pan and sauté the onion until just about tender. Add the carrots, cashews, tofu and ginger, and sauté about 3 minutes. Add the soya (soy) sauce, chilli pepper and cucumber and sauté about 2 minutes. Add the Pernod and coriander, sauté another 1 or 2 minutes and remove from the heat. Hold until ready to fill the tofu pockets.

Hot-and-Sour Beansprouts Filling	Hot-and-Sour Beansprouts Filling
4 oz (115g) mung beansprouts, coarsely chopped	2 cups mung beansprouts, coarsely chopped
3 radishes, sliced	3 radishes, sliced
½ cucumber, peeled and shredded	½ cucumber, peeled and shredded
1 oz (30g) chopped walnuts	¼ cup chopped walnuts
2 tablespoons chopped fresh coriander	2 tablespoons chopped fresh coriander
2 tablespoons crunchy peanut butter	2 tablespoons crunchy peanut butter
1 tablespoon dark soya sauce such as tamari or Kikkoman	1 tablespoon dark soy sauce such as tamari or Kikkoman
2 tablespoons cider or white wine vinegar	2 tablespoons cider or white wine vinegar
½ teaspoon hot red pepper powder or hot pepper oil	½ teaspoon hot red pepper powder or hot pepper oil
1½ teaspoons sesame oil	1½ teaspoons sesame oil
1 tablespoon safflower oil	1 tablespoon safflower oil
2 teaspoons freshly grated or minced ginger	2 teaspoons freshly grated or minced ginger
1 clove garlic, peeled	1 clove garlic, peeled
4 fl oz (120ml) Vegetable Stock (page 59) or Bouillon	½ cup Vegetable Stock (page 59) or Bouillon

1 Toss together the beansprouts, radishes, cucumber, walnuts and coriander leaves.

2 Place the remaining ingredients in a blender and blend together at high speed until smooth. Toss with the vegetables. Hold until ready to fill the tofu. This will keep for a day or two in the refrigerator.

Notes: Both filling recipes yield enough for 8 stuffed pockets. You could also serve these fillings as salads.

Curried Tofu and Vegetables

Serves 6 to 8.

Imperial (Metric)	American
2 tablespoons butter	2 tablespoons butter
1 tablespoon peanut or safflower oil	1 tablespoon peanut or safflower oil
1 teaspoon mustard seeds	1 teaspoon mustard seeds
1 teaspoon cumin seeds, crushed	1 teaspoon cumin seeds, crushed
½ teaspoon turmeric	½ teaspoon turmeric
½ teaspoon chilli powder	½ teaspoon chili powder
2 to 3 teaspoons curry powder, to taste	2 to 3 teaspoons curry powder, to taste
1 medium onion, sliced	1 medium onion, sliced
1 clove garlic minced or put through a press	1 clove garlic minced or put through a press
1 teaspoon minced fresh ginger	1 teaspoon minced fresh ginger
½ lb (250g) tofu, pressed if desired (see page 130) and diced	½ pound tofu, pressed if desired (see page 130) and diced
½ lb (250g) courgettes, sliced	½ pound zucchini, sliced
1 lb (½ kilo) cauliflower, broken into florets and sliced	1 pound cauliflower, broken into florets and sliced
½ lb (250g) custard marrow, sliced	½ pound yellow squash, sliced
2 oz (55g) raw peanuts, almonds or sunflower seeds	¼ cup raw peanuts, almonds or sunflower seeds
3 oz (85g) raisins	½ cup raisins
2 fl oz (60ml) water or vegetable stock	¼ cup water or vegetable stock
Sea salt and freshly ground pepper to taste	Sea salt and freshly ground pepper to taste
1 tablespoon cornflour or arrowroot dissolved in 1½ tablespoons water	1 tablespoon cornstarch or arrowroot dissolved in 1½ tablespoons water
8 fl oz (225ml) natural low-fat yogurt	1 cup plain low-fat yogurt
2 tablespoons chopped fresh coriander	2 tablespoons chopped fresh coriander

1 Heat the butter and oil together in a large, heavy-bottomed frying pan, casserole or wok and add the spices, onion, garlic and ginger. Sauté until the onion is tender and add the tofu. Sauté gently over a medium-low flame for 5 minutes, and add the courgettes (zucchini), cauliflower and marrow (squash). Cook, stirring, for 5 minutes. Add the raisins, nuts and water or stock, cover and simmer 5 to 10 minutes. Add sea salt and freshly ground pepper to taste, adjust seasonings and stir in the dissolved cornflour (starch) or arrowroot. Cook, stirring, until the vegetables are glazed, and remove from the heat.

2 Transfer to a serving dish and stir in the yogurt. Serve at once over hot, cooked grains, or with one of the pilafs on pages 139-144.

Dry Cooked, Spicy Tofu

Serves 4.

Use this as a stuffing for vegetables, as a side dish with grains and vegetables or even as a sandwich filling. It's supposed to have the dry texture and is based on an Indian dish traditionally made with meat.

Imperial (Metric)	American
2 tablespoons safflower or light vegetable oil	2 tablespoons safflower or light vegetable oil
1 onion, finely chopped	1 onion, finely chopped
2 to 3 cloves garlic, to taste, minced or put through a press	2 to 3 cloves garlic, to taste, minced or put through a press
1½ tablespoons minced fresh ginger	1½ tablespoons minced fresh ginger
1 small green chilli, seeded and minced	1 small green chili, seeded and minced
1 lb (500g) tofu, diced	1 pound tofu, diced
2 tablespoons soya sauce	2 tablespoons soy sauce
¼ teaspoon turmeric	¼ teaspoon turmeric
2 teaspoons Garam Masala (see page 26)	2 teaspoons Garam Masala (see page 26)
1 tablespoon lemon juice	1 tablespoon lemon juice
2 tablespoons chopped fresh coriander	2 tablespoons chopped fresh coriander

1 Heat the oil in a wide, heavy-bottomed frying pan and add the onions. Fry over medium heat until beginning to brown, about five minutes, stirring constantly.

2 Add the garlic, ginger and chilli and cook an additional two minutes. Add the tofu and mash with the back of your spoon. Add the soya (soy) sauce and cook, stirring, until the tofu begins to brown and is quite dry. Add the turmeric, stir for a moment and stir in the garam masala and lemon juice. The pan will be quite dry, but if you stir quickly the ingredients won't burn. Remove from the heat at once and stir in the coriander. Serve at once or use as a stuffing for vegetables.

Note: This will keep for 2 days in the refrigerator. It does not freeze, however.

North Indian Pilaf

Serves 6 to 8.
This recipe is adapted from Julie Sahni's 'Patiala Pilaf.'

Imperial (Metric)	American
14 oz (395g) basmati rice	**2 cups basmati rice**
1½ pints (1 litre) cold water	**4 cups cold water**
2 tablespoons vegetable oil	**2 tablespoons vegetable oil**
1 onion, chopped	**1 onion, chopped**
2 cloves garlic, minced or put through a press	**2 cloves garlic, minced or put through a press**
6 green cardamom pods	**6 green cardamom pods**
1 cinnamon stick, 3 inches (6cm) long	**1 cinnamon stick, 3 inches long**
8 whole cloves	**8 whole cloves**
½ teaspoon powdered ginger	**½ teaspoon powdered ginger**
2 bay leaves	**2 bay leaves**
1 teaspoon sea salt	**1 teaspoon sea salt**

 Wash the rice thoroughly in several rinses of cold water. Soak in the cold water for 30 minutes. Drain and retain the soaking liquid.

 Heat the oil in a large, lidded frying pan or wok and sauté the onion until tender. Add the garlic and sauté 1 minute, then add the spices and sauté another 30 seconds, stirring.

 Add the rice and more oil if necessary, and sauté, stirring, over moderate heat, until translucent and beginning to brown. Add the soaking liquid, sea salt and bay leaves, bring to a boil, stirring, then reduce heat and partially cover. Simmer 10 to 12 minutes, or until most of the water has evaporated and there are small steam holes covering the surface of the rice.

 Now cover the rice tightly and place the pan or wok on a wok ring, a flame-tamer or heat-resistant pad. Turn heat very low and continue to cook for 10 minutes, undisturbed. Turn off heat and allow rice to sit, undisturbed, another 5 minutes. Turn out onto a warm platter, surround with one of the vegetable dishes in Chapter 3 and serve.

Note: The whole spices are not meant to be eaten but will do no harm if they are.

Sweet Saffron Pilaf with Fruit

Serves 6 to 8.

Imperial (Metric)	American
14 oz (395g) basmati rice	2 cups basmati rice
1½ pints (1 litre) water	4 cups water
1 teaspoon saffron threads	1 teaspoon saffron threads
2 tablespoons safflower or vegetable oil	2 tablespoons safflower or vegetable oil
10 whole cloves	10 whole cloves
8 green cardamom pods	8 green cardamom pods
1 3-inch (6cm) stick cinnamon	1 3-inch stick cinnamon
3 oz (85g) raisins or sultanas	½ cup dark or golden raisins
3 oz (85g) chopped dried apricots	½ cup chopped dried apricots
2 tablespoons honey	2 tablespoons honey
1 teaspoon sea salt	1 teaspoon sea salt
4 tablespoons flaked blanched almonds	4 tablespoons slivered blanched almonds
4 ripe peaches, blanched, peeled and sliced	4 ripe peaches, blanched, peeled and sliced

 Wash the basmati rice thoroughly in several rinses of cold water. Place in a bowl and soak in the water for 30 minutes. Drain and retain the soaking water.

 Meanwhile crumble the saffron threads by mashing between your fingers or with the back of a spoon. Add two tablespoons warm water and continue to mash until the threads are dissolved.

 Heat the safflower oil in a large, lidded frying pan or wok and sauté the spices over medium heat for about 30 seconds. Add the drained rice and sauté, stirring, until the rice is translucent and beginning to toast. Add the liquid which you set aside, the saffron, sultanas (raisins), dried apricots, honey and sea salt. Bring to a boil, stirring, then reduce heat, cover partially and simmer 10 to 12 minutes, or until most of the water is absorbed and there are little steam holes in the surface of the rice.

4 Meanwhile brown the almonds in a little butter or in no butter, either in a dry frying pan or in a moderate oven. Set aside with the sliced peaches.

5 Now cover tightly and either place your pan or wok on a wok ring or on a flame-tamer or heat-resistant pad and turn the heat very low. Steam the pilaf, undisturbed, for 10 minutes. Turn off the heat and let sit without disturbing for another 5 minutes.

6 Transfer the pilaf to a warm platter, sprinkle the top with almonds and sliced peaches, and serve.

Note: The whole spices aren't meant to be eaten but won't harm you if they are.

Wheat Berry and Soya (Soy) Pilaf

Serves 4 to 6.

Imperial (Metric)	American
2¼ pints (750ml) Vegetable Stock (page 59) or Bouillon	3 cups Vegetable Stock (page 59) or Bouillon
2 tablespoons safflower or vegetable oil	2 tablespoons safflower or vegetable oil
1 clove garlic, minced or put through a press	1 clove garlic, minced or put through a press
½ medium-sized onion, minced	½ medium-sized onion, minced
2 teaspoons grated or minced fresh ginger	2 teaspoons grated or minced fresh ginger
½ lb (250g) mushrooms, cleaned, trimmed and sliced	½ pound mushrooms, cleaned, trimmed and sliced
1 teaspoon cumin seeds	1 teaspoon cumin seeds
½ lb (250g) whole wheat berries	1 cup whole wheat berries
2 oz (55g) soya flakes	½ cup soy flakes
4 fl oz (120ml) dry white wine or beer	½ cup dry white wine or beer
Sea salt and freshly ground pepper to taste	Sea salt and freshly ground pepper to taste
½ lb (250g) broccoli florets or courgettes, sliced	½ pound broccoli florets or zucchini, sliced
2 tablespoons chopped fresh parsley	2 tablespoons chopped fresh parsley

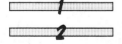

1 Have the stock simmering in a saucepan.

2 In a large, heavy-bottomed, lidded casserole heat one tablespoon of the oil and sauté the garlic and onion until the onion begins to soften. Add the ginger, mushrooms, and cumin seeds and continue to sauté another 3 minutes.

3   Add a little more oil and the wheat berries and soya (soy) flakes. Sauté, stirring, until the grains separate and begin to smell toasty, about 2 minutes. Add the wine or beer and cook, stirring, over medium heat until the liquid has just about been absorbed.

4   Add the stock or bouillon, stirring, and bring to a boil. Cover, reduce heat and simmer 45 minutes, checking after 30 minutes to make sure there is still enough liquid. Add more if the mixture seems dry or near-dry.

5   Add the broccoli or courgettes (zucchini), salt and freshly ground pepper to taste, and cover. Steam the vegetables with the grains for 5 to 10 minutes, to taste.

6   When the grains and vegetables are tender, pour off any excess cooking liquid, toss with the parsley and serve.

Broccoli and Cashew Pilaf

Serves 6 to 8.

Imperial (Metric)	American
5 oz (140g) raw cashews	1 cup raw cashews
2 tablespoons safflower or vegetable oil	2 tablespoons safflower or vegetable oil
2 teaspoons cumin seeds	2 teaspoons cumin seeds
1 small onion, minced	1 small onion, minced
2 cloves garlic, minced or put through a press	2 cloves garlic, minced or put through a press
2 teaspoons minced or grated fresh ginger	2 teaspoons minced or grated fresh ginger
1 bunch broccoli, separated into florets, stems peeled and sliced ¼ inch (5mm) thick	1 bunch broccoli, separated into florets, stems peeled and sliced ¼ inch thick
1 lb (500g) cooked brown rice or basmati rice	2½ cups cooked brown rice or basmati rice
1 teaspoon Mughal Garam Masala (page 25)	1 teaspoon Mughal Garam Masala (page 25)
Sea salt to taste	Sea salt to taste
2 oranges, peeled, white pith removed, and cut in rounds	2 oranges, peeled, white pith removed, and cut in rounds

Roast the cashews in a dry frying pan or a moderate oven until light brown. Set aside.

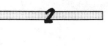

Heat the oil in a large, lidded frying pan or wok and add the cumin. Sauté over medium heat for about 20 seconds, stirring, then add the onion, garlic and ginger. Sauté, stirring, until the onion is tender and add the broccoli. Sauté, stirring, for about 2 minutes, and add ⅓ cup of water. Bring to a simmer, cover and simmer 8 to 10 minutes over medium-low heat, or until the broccoli is just tender.

Stir in the rice, cashews and Mughal Garam Masala and add sea salt to taste. Heat through, stirring, for about 5 minutes. Transfer to a warm platter, garnish with the oranges and serve.

Indian Fried Rice

Serves 6 to 8.

Imperial (Metric)	American
2 tablespoons safflower or vegetable oil	2 tablespoons safflower or vegetable oil
1 onion, chopped	1 onion, chopped
2 cloves garlic, minced or put through a press	2 cloves garlic, minced or put through a press
1 teaspoon minced fresh ginger	1 teaspoon minced fresh ginger
1 small head cauliflower or broccoli, broken into florets, stems peeled and sliced ¼ inch (½cm) thick	1 small head cauliflower or broccoli, broken into florets, stems peeled and sliced ¼ inch thick
2 carrots, peeled and sliced thin	2 carrots, peeled and sliced thin
1 lb (500g) cooked brown rice or basmati rice	2½ cups cooked brown rice or basmati rice
2 teaspoons ground roasted cumin seeds	2 teaspoons ground roasted cumin seeds
1 teaspoon ground roasted coriander	1 teaspoon ground roasted coriander
1 teaspoon Mughal Garam Masala (page 25)	1 teaspoon Mughal Garam Masala (page 25)
Sea salt to taste	Sea salt to taste
3 tablespoons chopped fresh coriander	3 tablespoons chopped fresh coriander

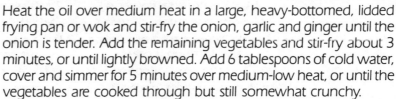

1 Heat the oil over medium heat in a large, heavy-bottomed, lidded frying pan or wok and stir-fry the onion, garlic and ginger until the onion is tender. Add the remaining vegetables and stir-fry about 3 minutes, or until lightly browned. Add 6 tablespoons of cold water, cover and simmer for 5 minutes over medium-low heat, or until the vegetables are cooked through but still somewhat crunchy.

2 Add the rice, sea salt to taste and the spices. Mix together well, and cover and cook over low heat for 5 minutes. Stir from time to time. (A thin layer of rice will probably stick to the bottom; it will detach easily with soaking.) Correct seasonings, stir in the fresh coriander and serve.

'Dirty' Rice

Serves 4 to 6.

Imperial (Metric)	American
For the Beans	**For the Beans**
½ lb (250g) red beans, washed, picked over and soaked	1 cup red beans, washed, picked over and soaked
1 onion, chopped	1 onion, chopped
3 cloves garlic, minced or put through a press	3 cloves garlic, minced or put through a press
1¼ pints (750ml) water	3 cups water
1 teaspoon sea salt	1 teaspoon sea salt
1 bay leaf	1 bay leaf
For the Rice	**For the Rice**
¾ teaspoon cayenne pepper	¾ teaspoon cayenne pepper
½ teaspoon sea salt (more or less to taste)	½ teaspoon sea salt (more or less to taste)
1 teaspoon ground black pepper	1 teaspoon ground black pepper
1¼ teaspoons sweet paprika	1¼ teaspoons sweet paprika
1 teaspoon dry mustard	1 teaspoon dry mustard
1 teaspoon ground cumin	1 teaspoon ground cumin
½ teaspoon dried thyme	½ teaspoon dried thyme
½ teaspoon oregano	½ teaspoon oregano
2 tablespoons safflower oil	2 tablespoons safflower oil
1 additional onion, chopped	1 additional onion, chopped
3 large cloves garlic, minced or put through a press	3 large cloves garlic, minced or put through a press
1 stick celery, chopped	1 stalk celery, chopped
1 green pepper, chopped	1 green pepper, chopped
½ lb (250g) brown rice	1 cup brown rice
¾ pint (500ml) cooking liquid from the beans	2 cups cooking liquid from the beans
8 fl oz (225ml) water	1 cup water

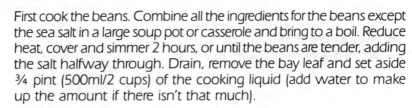

1 First cook the beans. Combine all the ingredients for the beans except the sea salt in a large soup pot or casserole and bring to a boil. Reduce heat, cover and simmer 2 hours, or until the beans are tender, adding the salt halfway through. Drain, remove the bay leaf and set aside ¾ pint (500ml/2 cups) of the cooking liquid (add water to make up the amount if there isn't that much).

2 Combine all the spices and herbs for the dirty rice in a small bowl.

3 Heat the safflower oil over medium-low heat in a large, heavy-bottomed casserole and add the onion and garlic. Sauté until the onion begins to soften and add the celery and green pepper. Continue to sauté, stirring, another minute or two and add the spice mixture. Sauté, stirring constantly, over medium-low heat for about 30 seconds, then add the rice, the beans and bean liquid you set aside and the water. Bring to a boil, reduce heat, cover and simmer 30 to 45 minutes, or until the rice is cooked al dente and most of the liquid absorbed (it can be a little soupy). Serve in bowls.

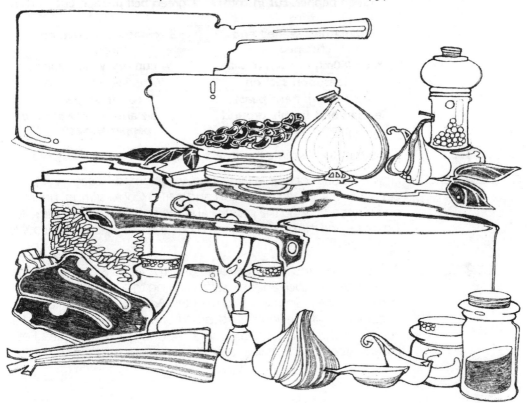

Spanish Rice

Serves 6.

Imperial (Metric)	American
1½ pints (1 litre) simmering Vegetable Stock (page 59)	1 quart simmering Vegetable Stock (page 59)
1 tablespoon butter or safflower oil	1 tablespoon butter or safflower oil
½ onion, minced	½ onion, minced
2 large cloves garlic, minced or put through a press	2 large cloves garlic, minced or put through a press
1 teaspoon sweet paprika	1 teaspoon sweet paprika
12 oz (340g) brown rice	1½ cups brown rice
1 green pepper, cut in thin strips	1 green bell pepper, cut in thin strips
3 tomatoes, seeded and chopped	3 tomatoes, seeded and chopped
2 fl oz (60ml) dry white wine	¼ cup dry white wine
½ teaspoon saffron	½ teaspoon saffron
6 oz (170g) fresh peas	1 cup fresh peas
Sea salt and freshly ground pepper to taste	Sea salt and freshly ground pepper to taste

1 Have the stock simmering in a saucepan.

2 Heat the butter or oil in a large, heavy-bottomed, lidded frying pan or casserole and add the onion and garlic. Cook, stirring, until the onion is tender. Add the paprika and the rice and cook, stirring, for 1 minute. Add the pepper and tomatoes and stir together for a couple of minutes.

3 Add the wine and continue to stir until the liquid is absorbed. Add the simmering stock and the saffron, bring to a second boil, cover and reduce heat. Simmer for 30 minutes. Add the peas and continue to cook until all the liquid is absorbed or until the rice is cooked al dente and the peas cooked through, about 10 more minutes. Pour off any stock that remains, correct seasonings and serve.

Sweet Couscous

Serves 8 generously.

Imperial (Metric)	American
12 oz (340g) couscous	2 cups couscous
1¼ pints (750ml) water	3 cups water
8 oz (250g) raisins	1¼ cups raisins
Boiling water to cover	Boiling water to cover
2 tablespoons butter	2 tablespoons butter
1 onion, chopped	1 onion, chopped
4 tablespoons flaked blanched almonds	4 tablespoons slivered blanched almonds
3 oz (85g) chopped dried apricots	½ cup chopped dried apricots
2 tablespoons cinnamon	2 tablespoons cinnamon
½ teaspoon turmeric	½ teaspoon turmeric
1 teaspoon ground ginger	1 teaspoon ground ginger
Sea salt to taste	Sea salt to taste
3 tablespoons honey	3 tablespoons honey
2 oranges, peeled, white membranes removed, chopped	2 oranges, peeled, white membranes removed, chopped

 Place the couscous in a bowl and pour on the water. Let sit while you prepare the remaining ingredients.

 Place the raisins in a bowl and pour on boiling water to cover. Let sit 15 minutes, then drain and retain the soaking water. Add water to measure 2 cups.

 Heat the butter in a heavy-bottomed, lidded saucepan, or in the bottom of a couscoussière. Sauté the onion over medium-low heat until it begins to turn golden. Add the raisins, almonds, dried apricots, spices, honey and soaking liquid from the raisins. Cover and simmer 25 to 30 minutes.

 Meanwhile rub the couscous between the palms of your hands, then place in the top part of the couscoussière or in a steamer above the simmering sauce and steam 25 to 30 minutes. Transfer to a platter and toss with the sweet, spicy sauce and the oranges. Serve at once.

Fallafels

Serves 6 to 8.

Imperial (Metric)	American
For the Croquettes	For the Croquettes
½ lb (250g) chick peas, washed, picked over and soaked	1 cup garbanzos, washed, picked over and soaked
Sea salt to taste	Sea salt to taste
2 fl oz (60ml) lemon juice	¼ cup lemon juice
2 fl oz (60ml) natural low-fat yogurt	¼ cup plain low-fat yogurt
2 large cloves garlic	2 large cloves garlic
6 heaped tablespoons sesame tahini	6 heaping tablespoons sesame tahini
½ teaspoon bicarbonate of soda	½ teaspoon baking soda
1 teaspoon ground cumin	1 teaspoon ground cumin
½ teaspoon ground coriander (more to taste)	½ teaspoon ground coriander (more to taste)
2 oz (55g) wholemeal pastry flour	½ cup whole wheat pastry flour
2 oz (55g) sesame seeds	½ cup sesame seeds
¼ teaspoon sea salt	¼ teaspoon sea salt
2 eggs	2 eggs
Safflower or peanut oil for deep-frying	Safflower or peanut oil for deep-frying
For the Rest of the Fallafel	For the Rest of the Fallafel
6 to 8 wholemeal pitta breads	6 to 8 whole wheat pita breads
3 ripe tomatoes, chopped	3 ripe tomatoes, chopped
1 small onion, chopped	1 small onion, chopped
1 small cucumber, chopped	1 small cucumber, chopped
½ oz (15g) chopped fresh parsley	½ cup chopped fresh parsley
1 clove garlic, minced or put through a press	1 clove garlic, minced or put through a press

Juice of 1 large lemon	Juice of 1 large lemon
Ground cayenne to taste	Ground cayenne to taste
¼ teaspoon chilli powder	¼ teaspoon chili powder
Sea salt and freshly ground pepper to taste	Sea salt and freshly ground pepper to taste
For the Yogurt-Tahini Spread	For the Yogurt-Tahini Spread
4 fl oz (120ml) natural low-fat yogurt	½ cup plain low-fat yogurt
3 tablespoons sesame tahini	3 tablespoons sesame tahini
Juice of ½ lemon	Juice of ½ lemon
1 clove garlic, minced or put through a press	1 clove garlic, minced or put through a press
Sea salt to taste	Sea salt to taste
Pinch of cayenne	Pinch of cayenne
Additional hot sauce (optional)	Additional hot sauce (optional)

Cook the beans in salted water until tender. Drain and purée with sea salt to taste, the lemon juice, yogurt, garlic, bicarbonate of (baking) soda, cumin and coriander. Let rest for 30 minutes. Meanwhile prepare the other ingredients. Chop the tomatoes, onion, cucumber and parsley and toss together with the garlic, lemon juice and spices. Season to taste with sea salt and freshly ground pepper. Set aside.

Roll the purée into balls about 2 inches in diameter, and set aside.

Start oil heating in a deep pan or wok. Mix together the flour and sesame seeds in a bowl or on a plate. Beat the eggs in another bowl.

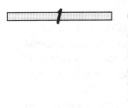

Dip the chick pea (garbanzo) balls into the egg, then coat lightly with the flour-sesame mixture and deep-fry in the oil until golden brown. Drain on paper towels. Keep warm in a low oven.

Mix together the ingredients for the yogurt sauce. Cut the pitta breads in half and spoon a little sauce into each half. Place a few balls in each half and top with the vegetable mixture. Serve, if you wish, with additional hot sauce on the side.

Spiced Yellow Mung Beans

Serves 4.
This is adapted from Julie Sahni's recipe.

Imperial (Metric)	American
½ lb (250g) yellow split mung beans, washed and picked over	1 cup yellow mung beans, washed and picked over
1 small onion, chopped	1 small onion, chopped
2 cloves garlic, minced or put through a press	2 cloves garlic, minced or put through a press
1 tablespoon safflower or vegetable oil	1 tablespoon safflower or vegetable oil
¼ teaspoon turmeric	¼ teaspoon turmeric
½ teaspoon grated fresh ginger	½ teaspoon grated fresh ginger
1 teaspoon sea salt	1 teaspoon sea salt
2 tablespoons additional safflower or vegetable oil	2 tablespoons additional safflower or vegetable oil
½ teaspoon black mustard seeds	½ teaspoon black mustard seeds
1 green chilli, seeded and chopped	1 green chili, seeded and chopped
1 tablespoon lemon juice	1 tablespoon lemon juice
2 tablespoons chopped fresh coriander	2 tablespoons chopped fresh coriander

1 Heat 1 tablespoon of oil over medium heat in a large, heavy-bottomed casserole and sauté the onion and garlic until the onion is tender. Add the beans, ginger, turmeric, sea salt and 1½ pints (1 litre/4 cups) water. Bring to a boil, stirring, reduce heat and simmer 30 minutes, stirring occasionally, or until the beans are tender. Mash the beans to a purée with the back of your spoon or with a wire whisk.

2 Heat the remaining oil in a frying pan over medium heat and add the mustard seeds. Stir a few seconds, or until they turn grey and stop spluttering, and add the chilli pepper. Stir for a moment, then stir into the bean purée along with the lemon juice and chopped fresh coriander. Correct seasonings and serve.

Note: This will keep for 2 to 3 days in a refrigerator and freezes well.

Chick Pea (Garbanzo Bean) Curry

Serves 6.

Imperial (Metric)	American
1 to 2 tablespoons safflower or vegetable oil	**1 to 2 tablespoons safflower or vegetable oil**
6 oz (170g) thinly sliced onion	**1 cup thinly sliced onion**
6 oz (170g) thinly sliced carrot	**1 cup thinly sliced carrot**
2 large cloves garlic, minced or put through a press	**2 large cloves garlic, minced or put through a press**
1½ tablespoons curry powder	**1½ tablespoons curry powder**
1 teaspoon Garam Masala (see page 26)	**1 teaspoon Garam Masala (see page 26)**
2 tomatoes, peeled and chopped	**2 tomatoes, peeled and chopped**
1 lb (500g) chick peas, cooked (save liquid)	**1 pound garbanzos, cooked (save liquid)**
Pinch of cayenne	**Pinch of cayenne**
Sea salt and freshly ground pepper to taste	**Sea salt and freshly ground pepper to taste**
1 to 2 tablespoons fresh lime juice, to taste	**1 to 2 tablespoons fresh lime juice, to taste**
1 tablespoon fresh chopped coriander	**1 tablespoon fresh chopped coriander**

1 Heat one tablespoon safflower oil in a large, heavy-bottomed skillet or wok over low heat and stir in the onion, garlic, ginger and spices. Cook gently for a few minutes and add the carrot. Continue to cook, stirring, until the onion is tender. Add more oil if necessary. Stir in the tomatoes, chick peas (garbanzos), enough of the reserved cooking liquid to cover them, cayenne and salt and freshly ground pepper to taste. Stir well and mash slightly with the back of a spoon.

2 Cook over medium heat for about 10 to 15 minutes, stirring from time to time, or until the beans are quite thick. Remove from the heat, add the lime juice and coriander and serve.

Sour Lentil Dahl

Serves 6.

Imperial (Metric)	American
10 oz (285g) pink or regular lentils, washed, picked over	1½ cups pink or regular lentils, washed, picked over
1 tablespoon chopped fresh ginger	1 tablespoon chopped fresh ginger
2 pints (1.25 litres) water	5 cups water
½ teaspoon turmeric	½ teaspoon turmeric
A 1-inch (2cm) ball of tamarind	A 1-inch ball of tamarind
8 fl oz (225ml) boiling water	1 cup boiling water
1 teaspoon sea salt	1 teaspoon sea salt
2 tablespoons safflower or vegetable oil	2 tablespoons safflower or vegetable oil
1 teaspoon cumin seeds	1 teaspoon cumin seeds
3 cloves garlic, minced or put through a press	3 cloves garlic, minced or put through a press
¼ teaspoon cayenne, more to taste	¼ teaspoon cayenne, more to taste

1 Combine the lentils, ginger, turmeric and 2 pints (1.25 litres/5 cups) water in a large saucepan or casserole and bring to a boil. Stir for a minute, reduce heat, cover and simmer 25 to 30 minutes, or until the lentils are soft.

2 Meanwhile place the tamarind in a small bowl and pour on one cup of boiling water. Allow to soak for 15 minutes, then mash with the back of a wooden spoon or your fingers. Strain, pressing all the fibres against the strainer to extract all the juice, and add the liquid to the lentils along with the sea salt.

3 Remove the cooked lentils from the heat and beat to a purée with a whisk or spoon (you can also thicken by puréeing a cup or 2 in a blender). Measure out 2½ pints (1.5 litres/6 cups) adding water if necessary. Correct salt.

4 Heat the safflower oil in a small frying pan and add the cumin seeds, garlic and cayenne. Sauté over medium-low heat just until the garlic is tender. Do not brown. Quickly stir into the lentil dahl and mix together well. Heat through, stirring, and serve.

Syrian Lentils with Noodles

Serves 6 to 8.

Imperial (Metric)	American
2 tablespoons safflower or vegetable oil	2 tablespoons safflower or vegetable oil
1 onion, chopped	1 onion, chopped
2 to 3 cloves garlic, to taste, minced or put through a press	2 to 3 cloves garlic, to taste, minced or put through a press
2 teaspoons ground roasted cumin	2 teaspoons ground roasted cumin
1 teaspoon ground roasted coriander	1 teaspoon ground roasted coriander
1 to 2 small cayenne peppers, to taste	1 to 2 small cayenne peppers, to taste
1 lb (500g) lentils, washed and picked over	2 cups lentils, washed and picked over
1 bay leaf	1 bay leaf
2¾ pints (1.75 litres) water	7 cups water
Sea salt and freshly ground pepper to taste	Sea salt and freshly ground pepper to taste
4 oz (250g) wholewheat spaghetti noodles, vermicelli or macaroni	4 ounces broken whole wheat spaghetti noodles, vermicelli or macaroni

1 Heat the oil in a large, heavy-bottomed casserole and sauté the onion with the garlic until the onion is tender. Add the cumin and coriander and continue to sauté another minute or so over medium heat.

2 Add the cayenne pepper, the lentils, bay leaf and water and bring to a boil. Add sea salt and pepper to taste, cover, reduce heat and simmer 45 minutes, or until the lentils are tender. Adjust seasonings.

3 Shortly before serving bring to a simmer and add the noodles. Cook until al dente (4 to 10 minutes depending on the kind of noodle) and serve at once in bowls.

Ginger-Flavoured Buckwheat Pasta

For 4 to 6 people.

Imperial (Metric)	American
2 oz (55g) buckwheat flour	½ cup buckwheat flour
4 oz (115g) wholemeal pastry or unbleached white flour	1 cup whole wheat pastry or unbleached white flour
2 teaspoons ground ginger	2 teaspoons ground ginger
¼ to ½ teaspoon sea salt, to taste	¼ to ½ teaspoon sea salt, to taste
2 eggs	2 eggs
1 teaspoon sesame oil	1 teaspoon sesame oil

1 *Using a food processor:* Place the flours, ginger and salt in the bowl of your food processor fitted with the steel blade and pulse several times to blend together. Add the eggs and sesame oil and process until the mixture is well blended. Take up the dough and press together, then knead for about 10 minutes by squeezing the dough from end to end, passing it from one hand to the other, or by slamming it down on a work surface, squeezing it, taking it up and slamming it down again. Dough will be soft and you might need to flour your hands a little bit. Wrap the dough in a plastic wrap and let rest for 30 minutes (dough can also be refrigerated at this point for a day to two, tightly wrapped in plastic).

2 *Mixing the dough by hand:* Sift together the flours, salt and ginger. Place on your work surface in a mound, then make a well in the centre. Break the eggs in the well and add the sesame oil. Gently beat the eggs together with a fork. Now begin brushing flour from the edges of the well into the eggs and incorporate in as much as you can with the fork. Use one hand to brush in the flour and to keep building up the edges of the well so that the eggs don't run out while you beat with the other. When most of the flour has been incorporated, gather up the dough and knead together. Brush away all the little balls of flour and egg which remain on the work surface. Knead the dough and proceed as above.

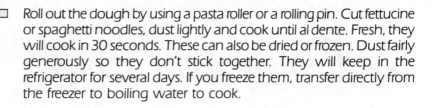

3 Roll out the dough by using a pasta roller or a rolling pin. Cut fettucine or spaghetti noodles, dust lightly and cook until al dente. Fresh, they will cook in 30 seconds. These can also be dried or frozen. Dust fairly generously so they don't stick together. They will keep in the refrigerator for several days. If you freeze them, transfer directly from the freezer to boiling water to cook.

Spicy Soba

Serves 4 to 6.

Imperial (Metric)	American
¾ lb (340g) buckwheat noodles or Ginger-flavoured Buckwheat Pasta (page 156)	¾ pound buckwheat noodles or Ginger-flavored Buckwheat Pasta (page 156)
1 tablespoon safflower or vegetable oil	1 tablespoon safflower or vegetable oil
2 teaspoons sea salt	2 teaspoons sea salt
3 tablespoons sesame oil	3 tablespoons sesame oil
½ to 1 teaspoon hot Chinese red pepper flakes or powder, to taste	½ to 1 teaspoon hot Chinese red pepper flakes or powder, to taste
1 tablespoon soya sauce	1 tablespoon soy sauce

Bring a large pot of water to a boil and add the safflower or vegetable oil and the sea salt. Add the noodles and cook until al dente, about 4 to 5 minutes. Drain and toss immediately with the remaining ingredients. Serve hot or cold.

5. Dairy and Eggs

Baked Tunisian Eggah

Serves 4 to 6.

Imperial (Metric)	American
3 tablespoons olive oil	3 tablespoons olive oil
4 cloves garlic, thinly sliced	4 cloves garlic, thinly sliced
1 onion, thinly sliced	1 onion, thinly sliced
1 sweet green pepper, seeded and thinly sliced	1 sweet green pepper, seeded and thinly sliced
1 sweet red pepper, seeded and thinly sliced	1 sweet red pepper, seeded and thinly sliced
2 courgettes, sliced about ¼ inch (½cm) thick	2 zucchini, sliced about ¼ inch thick
1 pound (500g) ripe tomatoes, peeled and cut in wedges	1 pound ripe tomatoes, peeled and cut in wedges
¼ to ½ teaspoon cayenne pepper, to taste	¼ to ½ teaspoon cayenne pepper, to taste
¾ teaspoon ground cumin	¾ teaspoon ground cumin
½ teaspoon ground coriander	½ teaspoon ground coriander
½ teaspoon cinnamon	½ teaspoon cinnamon
Sea salt and freshly ground pepper to taste	Sea salt and freshly ground pepper to taste
4 tablespoons chopped fresh parsley	4 tablespoons chopped fresh parsley
6 eggs	6 eggs

Heat the olive oil in a large, heavy-bottomed, lidded frying pan or casserole and add the onion and garlic. Sauté gently until the onion begins to soften. Add the green and red peppers and continue to sauté another 5 minutes, stirring. Add the courgettes (zucchini) and continue to sauté another 5 minutes. Stir in the tomatoes, spices and sea salt and freshly ground pepper to taste. Stir together, cover and reduce heat. Simmer gently for 30 to 40 minutes, or until the vegetables are cooked through and fragrant. If they begin to stick to the bottom of the pan add a little water. Correct seasonings and remove from the heat.

2 Meanwhile preheat the oven to 350 degrees F (180°C, gas mark 4) and oil or butter a baking dish large enough to accommodate the vegetables and eggs.

3 Beat the eggs in a large bowl and add the parsley. Stir in the vegetable mixture, correct seasonings again and turn into the prepared baking dish. Cover and bake 30 minutes. Remove the cover and bake another 10 minutes, or until the top is nicely browned and the eggs set. Serve at once.

Notes: You could also allow this to cool and serve, cut in squares, as an appetizer.

Scrambled Eggs with Hot Tomato Sauce

Serves 6 to 8.

Imperial (Metric)	American
2 tablespoons safflower or vegetable oil	2 tablespoons safflower or vegetable oil
1 onion, finely chopped	1 onion, finely chopped
3 cloves garlic, minced or put through a press	3 cloves garlic, minced or put through a press
1 tablespoon finely minced fresh ginger	1 tablespoon finely minced fresh ginger
1 hot green chilli, minced, or ¼ teaspoon cayenne	1 hot green chili, minced, or ¼ teaspoon cayenne
1 3-inch (7cm) stick cinnamon	1 3-inch stick cinnamon
8 green or white cardamom pods	8 green or white cardamom pods
2 teaspoons ground coriander	2 teaspoons ground coriander
½ teaspoon turmeric	½ teaspoon turmeric
1 lb (500g) tomatoes, peeled and finely chopped	1 pound tomatoes, peeled and finely chopped
1 teaspoon Garam Masala (see page 26)	1 teaspoon Garam Masala (see page 26)
¼ teaspoon freshly ground black pepper	¼ teaspoon freshly ground black pepper
Sea salt to taste	Sea salt to taste
8 eggs	8 eggs
3 tablespoons chopped fresh coriander	3 tablespoons chopped fresh coriander

1 Heat the oil in a large, heavy-bottomed frying pan and add the onion, garlic and ginger. Sauté over medium heat until the onion is tender. Add the hot chilli or cayenne, the cinnamon stick, cardamom, coriander and turmeric and stir together. Sauté about a minute and add the tomatoes, garam masala and pepper. Cook, stirring often, over medium heat for 20 minutes. Add sea salt to taste and correct seasonings. Turn heat very low.

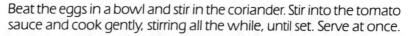 Beat the eggs in a bowl and stir in the coriander. Stir into the tomato sauce and cook gently, stirring all the while, until set. Serve at once.

Note: The hot tomato sauce can also be used as an omelette filling, or can be mixed with the eggs and the whole cooked as an eggah or Spanish omelette.

Curried Walnut and Apple Omelette

Serves 4.

Imperial (Metric)	American
1 tart apple, thinly sliced	1 tart apple, thinly sliced
1 tablespoon butter	1 tablespoon butter
1 teaspoon curry powder	1 teaspoon curry powder
½ teaspoon turmeric	½ teaspoon turmeric
¼ teaspoon ground ginger	¼ teaspoon ground ginger
6 eggs	6 eggs
4 oz (115g) chopped walnuts	¾ cup chopped walnuts
Sea salt and freshly ground pepper to taste	Sea salt and freshly ground pepper to taste

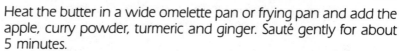 Heat the butter in a wide omelette pan or frying pan and add the apple, curry powder, turmeric and ginger. Sauté gently for about 5 minutes.

Beat the eggs in a bowl and stir in the walnuts, sea salt and freshly ground pepper to taste. Add to the pan and tilt the pan so that the egg spreads out in an even layer. Cook over medium-low heat, gently lifting the edges of the omelette and tilting the pan to let the eggs run underneath until the eggs are just about set, about 5 minutes.

Place the omelette under the grill (broiler) for a few minutes, or until the top of the omelette puffs and is cooked through. Serve at once, cut in wedges.

Puffed Yogurt Omelette

Serves 3 to 4.

This simple dish puffs up like a soufflé, and you don't even have to separate the eggs. It is intriguingly simple and has a very delicate flavour and texture.

Imperial (Metric)	American
6 eggs	**6 eggs**
8 fl oz (225ml) natural low-fat yogurt	**1 cup plain low-fat yogurt**
½ teaspoon curry powder	**½ teaspoon curry powder**
1 to 2 small fresh green chillies, seeded and minced (optional)	**1 to 2 small fresh green chillies, seeded and minced (optional)**
Sea salt to taste	**Sea salt to taste**
1 tablespoon butter	**1 tablespoon butter**
½ teaspoon ground roasted cumin (see page 14)	**½ teaspoon ground roasted cumin (see page 14)**
1 tablespoon chopped fresh coriander	**1 tablespoon chopped fresh coriander**

1 Beat together the eggs, yogurt, curry powder, optional chillies and sea salt to taste.

2 Heat the butter over medium-high heat in a 9- or 10-inch (23-25cm), preferably non-stick frying pan or omelette pan. When the butter stops sizzling, pour in the eggs. Swirl the pan to coat evenly. Keep swirling for about 30 seconds while you gently lift the edges of the omelette, allowing the eggs to run underneath.

3 Now sprinkle the top with the ground roasted cumin and the fresh coriander and turn the heat down to very low. Cover the pan with a lid or another pan turned upside down, and do not disturb for 5 to 7 minutes.

4 Uncover the pan (the omelette should be puffed, cook another few minutes if it is still uncooked on top.) and bring to the table at once. Slice in wedges and serve.

Steve's Migas

Serves 6.

Imperial (Metric)	American
12 eggs	12 eggs
Sea salt and freshly ground black pepper to taste	Sea salt and freshly ground black pepper to taste
4 fl oz (120ml) safflower or vegetable oil	½ cup safflower or vegetable oil
6 corn tortillas (may be stale), cut into strips	6 corn tortillas (may be stale), cut into strips
½ small onion, minced	½ small onion, minced
4 fresh or canned jalapeño or serrano peppers, seeded and chopped	4 fresh or canned jalapeño or serrano peppers, seeded and chopped
4 medium-sized tomatoes, seeded and chopped	4 medium-sized tomatoes, seeded and chopped
2 tablespoons butter	2 tablespoons butter
1 tablespoon chopped fresh coriander	1 tablespoon chopped fresh coriander

1 Beat the eggs lightly in a large bowl. Add sea salt and freshly ground pepper and set aside.

2 Heat the oil in a large, wide frying pan over high heat to 370 degrees F (190°C). Add the tortilla strips and fry until crisp and golden brown. This should only take a few seconds. Drain on paper towels.

3 Discard all but 2 tablespoons of the oil. Allow to cool for a few minutes. Reduce heat to low. Add the onions and peppers and sauté until the onions are soft but not brown. Add tomatoes and cook very briefly, about one minute. Season with a little sea salt, and transfer to a bowl.

4 Melt the butter in the frying pan and add the eggs. Cook slowly over low heat, stirring. When the eggs are somewhat set, stir in the vegetables. Just before the eggs are set, stir in the fried tortilla strips. Stir in the chopped, fresh coriander and serve at once.

Hard-Boiled Eggs and Tomatoes with Spices

Serves 4.

Imperial (Metric)	American
4 hard-boiled eggs, shelled, cut in half	4 hard-boiled eggs, shelled, cut in half
4 large ripe tomatoes, cut in wedges	4 large ripe tomatoes, cut in wedges
½ teaspoon each sea salt, Garam Masala (see page 26), ground coriander, ground cumin	½ teaspoon each sea salt, Garam Masala (see page 26), ground coriander, ground cumin
Freshly ground pepper	Freshly ground pepper
Chopped fresh parsley, chives or coriander for garnish	Chopped fresh parsley, chives or coriander for garnish

Arrange the eggs and tomatoes on a platter. Mix together the sea salt and spices and sprinkle over the eggs and tomatoes. Add a little freshly ground pepper and garnish with fresh parsley, chives or coriander. Serve as an hors d'oeuvre, a first course or as part of a light meal with other salads.

Curried Devilled Eggs

Serves 4.

Imperial (Metric)	American
4 large eggs, hard-boiled	4 large eggs, hard-boiled
Curry Mayonnaise (page 192), to taste	Curry Mayonnaise (page 192), to taste
Dijon style mustard to taste	Dijon style mustard to taste
Sweet paprika	Sweet paprika

Peel the eggs and cut in half. Gently remove the yolks and mash. Moisten to taste with Curry Mayonnaise (page 192) and Dijon-style mustard. Gently spoon or pipe back into the whites. Sprinkle with paprika and arrange on a platter. Serve chilled or at room temperature as an hors d'oeuvre.

Spiced Tomato Buttermilk

2½ cups.
This can be eaten as a cold soup or used as a sauce for rice.

Imperial (Metric)	American
1 tablespoon safflower or vegetable oil	1 tablespoon safflower or vegetable oil
4 cloves garlic, peeled and thinly sliced	4 cloves garlic, peeled and thinly sliced
½ hot green chilli pepper, minced	½ hot green chilli pepper, minced
¼ teaspoon cumin seeds	¼ teaspoon cumin seeds
1 large ripe tomato, peeled, seeded and chopped	1 large ripe tomato, peeled, seeded and chopped
6 fl oz (180ml) water	¾ cup water
Sea salt to taste	Sea salt to taste
8 fl oz (225ml) buttermilk	1 cup buttermilk
1 tablespoon chopped fresh coriander	1 tablespoon chopped fresh coriander

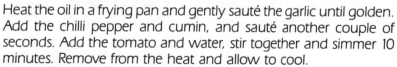

1 Heat the oil in a frying pan and gently sauté the garlic until golden. Add the chilli pepper and cumin, and sauté another couple of seconds. Add the tomato and water, stir together and simmer 10 minutes. Remove from the heat and allow to cool.

2 Stir the tomato mixture into the buttermilk. Add sea salt to taste and stir in the chopped fresh coriander. Serve over grains or as a cold soup.

Roasted Aubergine (Eggplant) Raita

This is adapted from a recipe by Madhur Jaffrey.

Imperial (Metric)	American
2 spring onions	2 green onions
¾ lb (340g) aubergine	¾ pound eggplant
¾ pint (500ml) natural low-fat yogurt	2 cups plain low-fat yogurt
1 clove garlic, minced or put through a press	1 clove garlic, minced or put through a press
¾ teaspoon ground cumin	¾ teaspoon ground cumin
½ teaspoon paprika	½ teaspoon paprika
3 tablespoons chopped fresh mint (optional)	3 tablespoons chopped fresh mint (optional)
Sea salt and freshly ground pepper to taste	Sea salt and freshly ground pepper to taste
Fresh lemon juice to taste (optional)	Fresh lemon juice to taste (optional)

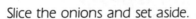

1   Slice the onions and set aside.

2   Preheat the oven to 450 degrees F (220°C, gas mark 7). Cut the aubergine (eggplant) in half lengthwise and score down to the skin but not through it, down the middle of the aubergine (eggplant). Place on an oiled baking sheet cut side down and bake in the preheated oven until thoroughly soft on the inside and charred on the outside, or about 30 minutes. Remove from the heat and allow to cool. Scrape out the flesh when cool enough to handle and discard the skin. Dice very small or mash.

3   Beat the yogurt with a whisk or fork until smooth. Stir in the aubergine (eggplant) and remaining ingredients. Season to taste with sea salt, chopped fresh mint, pepper and lemon juice. Chill or serve at room temperature.

Spicy Banana Raita

¾ pint/500ml/2 cups.

Imperial (Metric)	American
8 fl oz (225ml) natural low-fat yogurt	1 cup plain low-fat yogurt
½ to 1 fresh hot green chilli, to taste, minced	½ to 1 fresh hot green chili, to taste, minced
1 teaspoon mild-flavoured honey	1 teaspoon mild-flavored honey
1 firm, ripe banana, diced	1 firm, ripe banana, diced
Sea salt and freshly ground pepper to taste	Sea salt and freshly ground pepper to taste

Beat the yogurt with a whisk or fork until smooth. Stir in the remaining ingredients. Correct seasonings. Serve on the side with vegetable curries or over grains.

Spicy Cucumber Raita

Serves 4.
¾ pint/500ml/2 cups
This is adapted from a recipe by Madhur Jaffrey.

Imperial (Metric)	American
8 fl oz (225ml) natural low-fat yogurt	1 cup plain low-fat yogurt
⅛ teaspoon cayenne	⅛ teaspoon cayenne
2 tablespoons chopped fresh coriander	2 tablespoons chopped fresh coriander
1 teaspoon black mustard seeds, crushed	1 teaspoon black mustard seeds, crushed
1 medium-sized cucumber, peeled and grated	1 medium-sized cucumber, peeled and grated
Sea salt and freshly ground pepper to taste	Sea salt and freshly ground pepper to taste

Beat the yogurt until smooth with a whisk or fork. Add the remaining ingredients. Chill and serve with grains or vegetable curries.

Cucumber-Mint Raita

Serves 6.

Imperial (Metric)	American
¾ pint (500ml) natural low-fat yogurt	2 cups plain low-fat yogurt
1 medium-sized cucumber, peeled, seeded and minced	1 medium-sized cucumber, peeled, seeded and minced
2 to 3 tablespoons chopped fresh mint	2 to 3 tablespoons chopped fresh mint
¾ teaspoon ground roasted cumin	¾ teaspoon ground roasted cumin
¼ teaspoon chilli powder	¼ teaspoon chilli powder
Sea salt and freshly ground pepper to taste	Sea salt and freshly ground pepper to taste

Beat the yogurt in a bowl with a whisk or fork until smooth. Mix with the remaining ingredients. Serve as a side dish with curries and grains or as a salad or cold soup.

Spiced Cottage Cheese

¾-lb/340g/1½ cups.

Imperial (Metric)	American
½ lb (250g) cottage cheese	1 cup cottage cheese
6 tablespoons natural low-fat yogurt	⅓ cup plain low-fat yogurt
1¼ teaspoons Garam Masala (see page 26)	1¼ teaspoons Garam Masala (see page 26)
⅛ teaspoon cayenne	⅛ teaspoon cayenne
2 teaspoon lemon juice, or to taste	2 teaspoons lemon juice, or to taste

Blend together the cottage cheese and yogurt. Stir in the remaining ingredients. Correct seasonings. Use as a sandwich spread, especially good on dark sour bread, or as a dip for vegetables.

Leek and Potato Quiche with Cumin

Serves 6.

Imperial (Metric)	American
For the Pastry	For the Crust
4 oz (115g) wholemeal pastry flour	1 cup whole wheat pastry flour
2 oz (55g) cup unbleached white flour	½ cup unbleached white flour
2 oz (55g) wheat germ	½ cup wheat germ
½ teaspoon sea salt	½ teaspoon sea salt
6 oz (170g) cold unsalted butter	6 ounces cold unsalted butter
2 to 3 tablespoons ice-cold water	2 to 3 tablespoons ice-cold water
For the Filling	For the Filling
1 tablespoon butter	1 tablespoon butter
2 leeks, white part only, cleaned and thinly sliced	2 leeks, white part only, cleaned and thinly sliced
¾ lb (340g) new potatoes, diced	¾ pound new potatoes, diced
1 teaspoon crushed cumin seeds	1 teaspoon crushed cumin seeds
¼ teaspoon paprika	¼ teaspoon paprika
3 large eggs, at room temperature	3 large eggs, at room temperature
8 fl oz (225ml) milk	1 cup milk
2 tablespoons dried milk	2 tablespoons dried milk
¼ teaspoon sea salt	¼ teaspoon sea salt
Pinch of freshly grated nutmeg	Pinch of freshly grated nutmeg
Freshly ground pepper to taste	Freshly ground pepper to taste
4 oz (115g) Gruyère cheese, grated	4 ounces Gruyère cheese, grated
2 oz (55g) Parmesan cheese, grated	2 ounces Parmesan cheese, grated
Freshly ground pepper	Freshly ground pepper

1 First make the pastry base (pie crust). Mix together the flours, wheat germ and sea salt and cut in the butter. Add the water and gather into a ball. Wrap in plastic wrap and chill at least one hour and preferably overnight. Roll out and line a 12-inch (30cm) quiche pan. Pinch an attractive lip around the edge. Trim excess pastry and save for another purpose.

2 Preheat the oven to 350 degrees F (180°C, gas mark 4). Prick the pastry in several places with a fork and prebake 5 minutes. Remove from the heat.

3 Steam the potatoes until tender, about 10 minutes, and set aside.

4 Heat the butter in a frying pan and add the leeks. Sauté until they begin to soften and add the cumin, potatoes and paprika. Continue to sauté another 5 minutes and remove from the heat.

5 Blend together the eggs, milk, dry milk, nutmeg and freshly ground pepper in a blender.

6 Toss the cheeses together with the leeks and potatoes. Line the prebaked base (crust) with this mixture. Place in the oven and bake 30 to 40 minutes, or until firm to the touch and beginning to brown on top. Remove from the heat, let sit about 5 minutes, and serve.

Corn Pudding

Serves 4.

Imperial (Metric)	American
1 tablespoon butter	1 tablespoon butter
1 small onion, minced	1 small onion, minced
1 green pepper, chopped	1 green pepper, chopped
1 teaspoon crushed cumin seeds	1 teaspoon crushed cumin seeds
¼ teaspoon chilli powder	¼ teaspoon chili powder
1 canned or fresh jalapeño, seeded and chopped	1 canned or fresh jalapeño, seeded and chopped
12 oz (340g) fresh sweetcorn kernels, coarsely, puréed	2 cups fresh corn kernels, coarsely puréed
4 fl oz (120ml) milk	½ cup milk
4 eggs	4 eggs
½ teaspoon sweet paprika	½ teaspoon sweet paprika
Sea salt and freshly ground pepper to taste	Sea salt and freshly ground pepper to taste

1 Preheat the oven to 375 degrees F (190°C, gas mark 5). Butter a 3 pint (2 litre/2-quart) soufflé dish.

2 Heat the butter in a heavy-bottomed frying pan and sauté the onion and green pepper until the onion is tender, or about 3 minutes. Add the cumin seeds, chilli powder, jalapeño and corn kernels and continue to sauté, stirring, for another 3 minutes. Remove from the heat.

3 Separate 2 of the eggs. Beat together the whole eggs, egg yolks and milk. Add the corn mixture, paprika and salt and freshly ground pepper to taste.

4 Beat the egg whites until they form stiff peaks and fold into the corn mixture. Carefully turn into the buttered soufflé dish and bake for 30 minutes, or until the top is browned and the mixture set.

6. Mexican and Tex-Mex Dishes

Salsa Fresca

About ⅔ pint (340ml/1½ cups).

Imperial (Metric)	American
1 lb (500g) ripe tomatoes, chopped	1 pound ripe tomatoes, chopped
½ small onion, minced	½ small onion, minced
3 tablespoons chopped fresh coriander	3 tablespoons chopped fresh coriander
2 serrano or jalapeño peppers, fresh or tinned, seeded (use rubber gloves) and minced	2 serrano or jalapeño peppers, fresh or canned, seeded (use rubber gloves) and minced
2 tablespoons red wine vinegar	2 tablespoons red wine vinegar
Sea salt to taste	Sea salt to taste

Mix together all the ingredients in a bowl and serve, or chill and serve. This will hold for a day or two.

Green Tomato Sauce

¾ pint (600ml/2 cups).

Imperial (Metric)	American
1 lb (500g) green Mexican tomatoes, available in Mexican groceries and some supermarkets and markets	**1 pound green Mexican tomatoes, available in Mexican groceries and some produce markets and supermarkets**
2 fresh serrano peppers or tinned jalapeños	**2 fresh serrano peppers or canned jalapeños**
2 cloves garlic, minced or put through a press	**2 cloves garlic, minced or put through a press**
½ medium onion, minced	**½ medium onion, minced**
1 tablespoon safflower or vegetable oil	**1 tablespoon safflower or vegetable oil**
Sea salt to taste	**Sea salt to taste**

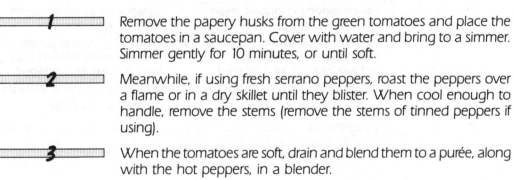

1 Remove the papery husks from the green tomatoes and place the tomatoes in a saucepan. Cover with water and bring to a simmer. Simmer gently for 10 minutes, or until soft.

2 Meanwhile, if using fresh serrano peppers, roast the peppers over a flame or in a dry skillet until they blister. When cool enough to handle, remove the stems (remove the stems of tinned peppers if using).

3 When the tomatoes are soft, drain and blend them to a purée, along with the hot peppers, in a blender.

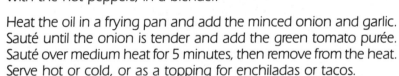

4 Heat the oil in a frying pan and add the minced onion and garlic. Sauté until the onion is tender and add the green tomato purée. Sauté over medium heat for 5 minutes, then remove from the heat. Serve hot or cold, or as a topping for enchiladas or tacos.

Mexican-Style Beans

Serves 4 to 6.

Imperial (Metric)	American
1 lb (500g) borlotti beans, washed, picked over and soaked	1 pound pinto beans, washed, picked over and soaked
1 onion, chopped	1 onion, chopped
4 cloves garlic, minced or put through a press	4 cloves garlic, minced or put through a press
1 tablespoon safflower or vegetable oil	1 tablespoon safflower or vegetable oil
2½ pints (1.5 litres) water	6 cups water
1 to 2 tinned or fresh jalapeño peppers, to taste, cut in half, seeds and membranes removed	1 to 2 canned or fresh jalapeño peppers, to taste, cut in half, seeds and membranes removed
2 sprigs epazote, if available	2 sprigs epazote, if available
1 teaspoon ground cumin	1 teaspoon ground cumin
Sea salt to taste	Sea salt to taste
4 to 5 tablespoons fresh chopped coriander	4 to 5 tablespoons fresh chopped coriander

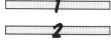 Soak the beans overnight and drain.

 Heat the oil in a large, heavy-bottomed bean pot or casserole and sauté the onion with half the garlic until tender. Add the beans, water, peppers, epazote and cumin. Bring to a boil, cover, reduce heat and simmer one hour.

Add the sea salt, coriander and remaining garlic and continue to simmer another hour, or until the beans are tender and the broth aromatic. Serve with fresh corn tortillas, rice or cornbread.

Note: These freeze well and will keep for 2 to 3 days in the refrigerator.

Refried Beans

Serves 4 to 6.

Imperial (Metric)	American
1 lb (½ kilo) borlotti or black beans, washed, picked over and soaked overnight	1 pound pinto or black beans, washed, picked over and soaked overnight
1 onion, chopped	1 onion, chopped
4 cloves garlic, minced or put through a press	4 cloves garlic, minced or put through a press
1 tablespoon safflower or vegetable oil	1 tablespoon safflower or vegetable oil
2½ pints (1½ litres) water	6 cups water
Sea salt to taste	Sea salt to taste
4 tablespoons chopped fresh coriander	4 tablespoons chopped fresh coriander
2-3 tablespoons additional safflower or vegetable oil	2-3 tablespoons additional safflower or vegetable oil
1 tablespoon ground chilli powder	1 tablespoon ground chili powder
1 tablespoon ground cumin	1 tablespoon ground cumin

1 First cook the beans. Heat 1 tablespoon of oil in a large, heavy-bottomed soup pot or casserole and sauté the onion and half the garlic until tender. Drain the beans and add along with the water. Bring to a boil, reduce heat, cover and simmer one hour.

2 Add sea salt to taste and the remaining garlic and coriander and simmer another hour, or until tender.

3 Drain the beans and retain about half the cooking liquid. Purée ⅔ of the beans in a food processor or blender, not until smooth but leaving some texture. Use some of the cooking liquid to moisten. You can also mash the beans with the back of a spoon or with a potato masher as you fry them.

4 Heat one tablespoon of the oil in a large, heavy-bottomed frying pan (nonstick is good here) and add half the cumin and chilli powder. Sauté a minute, then add half the puréed beans and half the whole beans. Sauté, stirring and mashing with the back of your spoon, for about 15 to 20 minutes or longer, adding a little cooking liquid if they seem too dry. They should bubble while a crust forms on the bottom and they develop a kind of toasty aroma. Transfer an ovenproof casserole and repeat this step with the remaining ingredients. Correct seasonings and keep warm in a low oven.

Note: These freeze well and will keep for two to three days in the refrigerator.

Bean Burritos

Serves 6.

Imperial (Metric)	American
6 wholemeal tortillas (available in natural food stores)	**6 whole wheat flour tortillas (available in natural food stores)**
1 lb (500g) cooked Mexican-Style Beans (page 175)	**2 cups cooked Mexican-Style Beans (page 175)**
1 teaspoon ground cumin	**1 teaspoon ground cumin**
1 teaspoon chilli powder	**1 teaspoon chili powder**
1 tablespoon safflower, corn or vegetable oil	**1 tablespoon safflower, corn or vegetable oil**
2 oz (55g) grated Cheddar cheese	**2 ounces grated Cheddar or Monterey Jack cheese**
1 oz (30g) shredded lettuce or alfalfa sprouts	**1 cup shredded lettuce or alfalfa sprouts**
2 to 3 tomatoes, chopped	**2 to 3 tomatoes, chopped**

1 Preheat the oven to 325 degrees F (170°C, gas mark 3 to 4). Wrap the tortillas in foil and place in the oven while you prepare the beans.

2 Drain the beans, retaining about 4 fl oz (120ml/½ cup) of their liquid. Coarsely purée, using the pulse action, in a food processor or blender, along with the cumin and chilli powder. Moisten with the bean broth.

3 Heat the oil in a large frying pan (skillet) and add the beans. Sauté, stirring, about 10 minutes.

4 Remove the tortillas from the oven and spread the refried beans down the centre. Top with the cheese and roll up. Heat in the oven for about 15 to 20 minutes, or until the cheese melts. Serve with the chopped tomatoes and lettuce on the side.

Meatless Chilli

Serves 4 to 6.

Imperial (Metric)	American
2 onions, chopped	2 onions, chopped
4 large cloves garlic, minced or put through a press	4 large cloves garlic, minced or put through a press
1 tablespoon safflower oil	1 tablespoon safflower oil
2 large carrots, chopped or grated	2 large carrots, chopped or grated
1 large pepper, chopped	1 large bell pepper, chopped
2 large tins tomatoes, drained and chopped, or 3 lbs (1.5 kilos) fresh ripe tomatoes, chopped	2 large cans tomatoes, drained and chopped, or 3 pounds fresh ripe tomatoes, chopped
1 small tin tomato purée	1 small can tomato paste
1 bay leaf	1 bay leaf
1 tablespoon chili powder	1 tablespoon chili powder
2 teaspoons cumin	2 teaspoons cumin
2 dried cayenne peppers, or ¼ teaspoon cayenne pepper	2 dried cayenne peppers, or ¼ teaspoon cayenne pepper
1 or 2 dried poblano chillies, if available (optional)	1 or 2 dried poblano chillies, if available (optional)
Sea salt and freshly ground pepper to taste	Sea salt and freshly ground pepper to taste
1 lb (500g) red or kidney beans, cooked (may use tinned)	1 pound red or kidney beans, cooked (may use canned)
4 fl oz (120ml) liquid from the beans	½ cup of the liquid from the beans
1 teaspoon oregano	1 teaspoon oregano

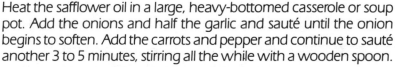

1 Heat the safflower oil in a large, heavy-bottomed casserole or soup pot. Add the onions and half the garlic and sauté until the onion begins to soften. Add the carrots and pepper and continue to sauté another 3 to 5 minutes, stirring all the while with a wooden spoon.

2 Add the tomatoes, tomato purée (paste), bay leaf and spices and bring to a simmer. Crumble in the optional dried poblano pepper and add the remaining garlic. Reduce heat, cover and simmer over very low heat, stirring occasionally, for 30 minutes. Stir in the beans

and their liquid and the oregano and continue to cook another 30 minutes. Check from time to time and stir to be sure that the chilli doesn't stick. Adjust seasonings, adding salt, pepper, garlic or cayenne to taste.

3 Serve with cornbread or corn tortillas or with whole wheat bread and a big green salad.

Spiced Nacho Chips

24 chips.

The nacho chips you make at home will taste much better than the ones that come out of a bag. You need a tortilla press and a heavy cast iron skillet, or even better, a *comal*, or Mexican griddle, for these. Masa Harina is a special kind of cornmeal for corn tortillas.

Imperial (Metric)	American
2 cloves garlic, peeled and sliced very thin	2 cloves garlic, peeled and sliced very thin
1 tablespoon safflower or vegetable oil	1 tablespoon safflower or vegetable oil
½ lb (250g) masa harina	2 cups masa harina
1 oz (30g) unbleached white flour	¼ cup unbleached white flour
½ teaspoon sea salt	½ teaspoon sea salt
½ teaspoon ground cumin	½ teaspoon ground cumin
½ teaspoon chilli powder	½ teaspoon chili powder
8 fl oz (225ml) plus 2 to 3 tablespoons water, as needed	1 cup plus 2 to 3 tablespoons water, as needed
2 plastic bags	2 plastic bags
1½ pints (1 litre) safflower, vegetable or corn oil for deep-frying	1 quart safflower, vegetable or corn oil for deep-frying

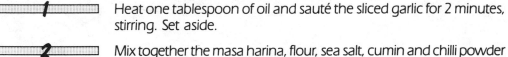

1 Heat one tablespoon of oil and sauté the sliced garlic for 2 minutes, stirring. Set aside.

2 Mix together the masa harina, flour, sea salt, cumin and chilli powder in a bowl. Stir in the sautéed garlic. Pour in 8 fl oz (1 cup) of the water all at once and mix together quickly with your hands. Dough should not be in a big lump but should be slightly crumbly and not too dry. If the dough seems too dry add a little water, a tablespoon at a time. Let rest for 15 minutes.

3 Take up small marble-sized pieces of the dough and shape into little balls.

 **4** Heat a *comal* griddle or heavy-bottomed frying pan over medium-high heat. To press out the tortilla chips place one of the plastic bags on your tortilla press and one, two or three balls, widely spaced, on top of this. Press down a little with your thumb, and place the other plastic bag on top. Now press the tortillas, being careful not to press too hard or your tortilla chips will be too thin. Lift the press and peel off the top bag. Flip the tortillas gently onto the peeled-off bag, and peel off the bottom bag.

 **5** Transfer the little tortillas to the hot *comal* or frying pan and cook about 1 minute, or until the tortillas are just beginning to dry around the edges. Turn and cook another minute. Remove from the heat.

 **6** To make the final chips, heat the oil to 370 degrees F (190°C) in a deep frying pan, saucepan or wok and add the chips, a few at a time. Deep-fry until crisp and golden. This should only take a few seconds. Drain on paper towels and toss with sea salt to taste.

Guacomole Nachos

24 to 30 nachos.

Imperial (Metric)	American
8 corn tortillas	8 corn tortillas
Oil for deep-frying	Oil for deep-frying
2 ripe avocados	2 ripe avocados
1 small ripe tomato, chopped	1 small ripe tomato, chopped
1 small clove garlic, minced or put through a press	1 small clove garlic, minced or put through a press
1 tablespoon finely minced onion	1 tablespoon finely minced onion
¼ teaspoon ground cumin	¼ teaspoon ground cumin
¼ teaspoon chilli powder	¼ teaspoon chilli powder
Juice of 1 large lemon	Juice of 1 large lemon
Sea salt to taste	Sea salt to taste
2 oz (55g) Cheddar cheese, grated	2 ounces Cheddar cheese, grated
6 tablespoons natural low-fat yogurt	⅓ cup plain low-fat yogurt
4 tablespoons Salsa Fresca (page 173)	4 tablespoons Salsa Fresca page 173)

 Cut the tortillas into quarters. Heat the oil to 360 degrees F (180°C) and deep-fry until crisp and golden. This should only take a few seconds. Drain on paper towels.

 Mash together the avocados, tomato, garlic and onion. Season with the cumin, chilli powder, lemon juice and sea salt to taste.

 Heat the grill (broiler). Sprinkle the grated cheese over the chips and melt under the grill (broiler). When thoroughly melted, remove the chips and spoon on the guacamole, top with a small spoonful of plain low-fat yogurt and garnish with salsa fresca. Serve.

Bean Nachos

24 nachos.

Imperial (Metric)	American
6 corn tortillas	**6 corn tortillas**
Safflower or vegetable oil for deep-frying	**Safflower or vegetable oil for deep-frying**
½ lb (250g) Refried Beans (page 176)	**1 cup Refried Beans (page 176)**
2 oz (55g) Cheddar cheese, grated	**2 ounces Cheddar or Monterey Jack cheese, grated**
4 tinned jalapeño chillies, cut in rounds	**4 canned jalapeño chilies, cut in rounds**

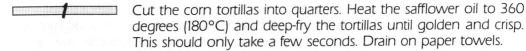

Cut the corn tortillas into quarters. Heat the safflower oil to 360 degrees (180°C) and deep-fry the tortillas until golden and crisp. This should only take a few seconds. Drain on paper towels.

Preheat the grill (broiler). Place 2 heaped teaspoons of the refried beans on each nacho chip. Sprinkle the cheese over the beans and grill (broil) briefly to melt the cheese. Garnish with a round of jalapeño pepper and serve.

Bean and Avocado Chalupas

Serves 4 to 6.

Imperial (Metric)	American
1 recipe Refried Beans (page 176)	1 recipe Refried Beans (page 176)
2 large or 3 small, ripe avocados, preferably the dark, knobby Haas variety	2 large or 3 small, ripe avocados, preferably the dark, knobby Haas variety
1 small serrano pepper, minced	1 small serrano pepper, minced
4 tomatoes, chopped	4 tomatoes, chopped
Juice of 1 lemon	Juice of 1 lemon
1 small onion, minced	1 small onion, minced
1 small clove garlic, minced or put through a press	1 small clove garlic, minced or put through a press
½ teaspoon ground cumin	½ teaspoon ground cumin
½ teaspoon chilli powder	½ teaspoon chili powder
Sea salt to taste	Sea salt to taste
1 tablespoon red wine vinegar	1 tablespoon red wine vinegar
1 to 2 additional serrano or jalapeño peppers, chopped	1 to 2 additional serrano or jalapeño peppers, chopped
3 to 4 tablespoons chopped fresh coriander	3 to 4 tablespoons chopped fresh coriander
6 oz (170g) Cheddar cheese, grated	6 ounces Cheddar cheese, grated
3 oz (85g) shredded lettuce	1½ cups shredded lettuce
8 to 12 flat corn tortilla crisps (chalupa crisps). (You can deep-fry your own corn tortillas if you can't find tortilla crisps.)	8 to 12 flat corn tortilla crisps (chalupa crisps). (You can deep-fry your own corn tortillas if you can't find tortilla crisps.)

 Make the refried beans and set aside (keep warm in a medium oven if you are serving the chalupas soon).

 Mash the avocados together with one of the tomatoes, one chopped serrano pepper, a quarter of the onions (more to taste), the garlic, cumin, chilli powder, lemon juice and sea salt to taste. Correct seasonings, adding more lemon juice or spices if you wish.

 Chop the remaining 3 tomatoes and toss with the remaining onion, the vinegar, chopped serranos or jalapeno, chopped fresh coriander and sea salt to taste.

 Have all the ingredients in separate bowls. To assemble the chalupas, spread a generous spoonful of refried beans on each tortilla crisp, top with the avocado purée, then some grated cheese, shredded lettuce and the tomato salsa.

Stuffed Jalapeños

Serves 4 to 6.

Imperial (Metric)	American
6 tinned pickled jalapeño peppers	**6 canned pickled jalapeño peppers**
¼ lb (115g) ricotta cheese	**¼ pound ricotta cheese**
¼ lb (115g) goat's cheese	**¼ pound goat's cheese**
¼ teaspoon ground cumin	**¼ teaspoon ground cumin**
Chopped fresh coriander as garnish	**Chopped fresh coriander as garnish**

 Wear rubber gloves as the peppers will irritate your hands. Cut the jalapeños in half and discard the seeds.

 Mash the two cheeses together in a bowl and stir in the cumin. Put the mixture into a pastry bag and pipe it into the jalapeño shells (or fill them with a spoon). Arrange on a plate and garnish with the coriander.

Green Rice with Stuffed Chillies

Serves 6.

Imperial (Metric)	American
1 oz (30g) parsley	1 cup parsley
¼ oz (7g) fresh coriander leaves	¼ cup fresh coriander leaves
3 fl oz (90ml) water	⅓ cup water
½ small onion, minced	½ small onion, minced
2 cloves garlic, minced or put through a press	2 cloves garlic, minced or put through a press
2 tablespoons safflower or vegetable oil	2 tablespoons safflower or vegetable oil
10 oz (285g) brown rice, preferably long grain, washed	1¼ cups brown rice, preferably long grained, washed
1¼ pints (750ml) water or Vegetable Stock (page 59)	3 cups water or Vegetable Stock (page 59)
8 fl oz (225ml) milk	1 cup milk
½ to 1 teaspoon sea salt, to taste	½ to 1 teaspoon sea salt, to taste
12 tinned jalapeños, drained	12 canned jalapeños, drained
¾ lb (340g) mild Cheddar cheese, grated	¾ pound mild Cheddar cheese, grated
½ to 1 teaspoon ground cumin, to taste	½ to 1 teaspoon ground cumin, to taste

 Blend together the parsley, coriander leaves and water in a blender. Set aside.

 Heat the oil in a large, heavy-bottomed, lidded frying pan or casserole and add the onion and garlic. Sauté over medium heat until the onion is tender. Add the rice and sauté, stirring about 5 minutes. Stir in the blended parsley and coriander and combine well.

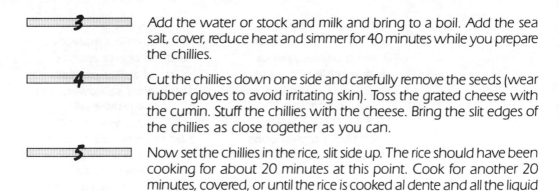

3 Add the water or stock and milk and bring to a boil. Add the sea salt, cover, reduce heat and simmer for 40 minutes while you prepare the chillies.

4 Cut the chillies down one side and carefully remove the seeds (wear rubber gloves to avoid irritating skin). Toss the grated cheese with the cumin. Stuff the chillies with the cheese. Bring the slit edges of the chillies as close together as you can.

5 Now set the chillies in the rice, slit side up. The rice should have been cooking for about 20 minutes at this point. Cook for another 20 minutes, covered, or until the rice is cooked al dente and all the liquid absorbed.

Mole Sauce

About 1½ pints (1 litre/1 quart).
This is a rich Mexican sauce made with several kinds of dried chilli peppers, spices, nuts, raisins and even a little bit of chocolate. If you've never eaten mole (pronounced 'molay,'), this recipe might look strange, but if you like complex, richly-seasoned food you will love this. It is fairly time-consuming, but it's worth the effort. No spice cookbook would be complete without this recipe. My vegetarian version is quite a bit different from the authentic mole, which is made with a fearful amount of lard and calls for turkey stock rather than vegetable stock. But the richness of the spices comes through here, and that's the important thing. Mole is usually served with turkey or chicken. I serve it with cheese enchiladas (see recipe, page 190), with hot, cooked grains, as a dip for raw vegetables and even as a spread.

Note: If you can't get the chilli peppers listed here, use a different combination of those chillies you can get. The flavour will be slightly different, but it will still be mole.

Continued over page

Imperial (Metric)	American
8 dried chillies mulatos	8 dried chilies mulatos
5 dried chillies anchos	5 dried chilies anchos
6 dried chillies pasillas	6 dried chilies pasillas
4 tablespoons safflower, corn or vegetable oil	4 tablespoons safflower, corn or vegetable oil
8 fl oz (225ml) water	1 cup water
2 additional tablespoons safflower, corn or vegetable oil	2 additional tablespoons safflower, corn or vegetable oil
10 peppercorns	10 peppercorns
¼ teaspoon toasted cumin seeds	¼ teaspoon toasted cumin seeds
¼ teaspoon toasted coriander seeds	¼ teaspoon toasted coriander seeds
½ teaspoon cinnamon, or ½-inch (1cm) stick	½ teaspoon cinnamon, or ½-inch stick
1 tablespoon reserved chilli seeds, toasted	1 tablespoon reserved chili seeds, toasted
4 tablespoons sesame seeds, toasted	4 tablespoons sesame seeds, toasted
1 large ripe tomato, peeled	1 large ripe tomato, peeled
3 cloves garlic, toasted in a dry frying pan until brown and set aside	3 cloves garlic, toasted in a dry frying pan until brown and set aside
1 additional tablespoon safflower, corn or vegetable oil	1 additional tablespoon safflower, corn or vegetable oil
2 tablespoons raisins	2 tablespoons raisins
30 almonds	30 almonds
4 pieces toasted or stale French or wholemeal bread	4 pieces toasted or stale French or whole wheat bread
1 stale corn tortilla	1 stale corn tortilla
1½ oz (45g) Mexican or bitter chocolate	1½ ounces Mexican or bitter chocolate
1½ to 2 pints (1 to 1.25 litres) Vegetable Stock or Bouillon (pages 59 and 60)	4 to 5 cups Vegetable Stock or Bouillon (pages 59 and 60)
Sea salt to taste	Sea salt to taste

1 *The Day Before:* Split open the chillies and remove the seeds and membranes, retaining 1 tablespoon of the seeds for future use. Heat the first 4 tablespoons of the oil and sauté the chillies for about 2 minutes, being very careful not to burn them. Remove from the heat, place in a bowl and cover with warm water. Soak overnight (you can toast the chilli seeds and the spices during this time).

2 Drain the chillies and purée in a blender with 8 fl oz (1 cup) of water. Heat the next 2 tablespoons oil in a large, heavy-bottomed frying pan and sauté the chilli paste, stirring over medium-high heat, for 10 minutes. The mixture will splutter and you should use a lid to protect yourself. Set aside.

3 Grind together all the spices, along with the toasted chilli seeds, in a spice mill. Transfer to a blender along with the tomato, garlic and sesame seeds (a blender works better than a food processor here for achieving the correct texture).

4 Heat the remaining tablespoon of oil and sauté the raisins just until they plump. Transfer, using a slotted spoon, to the blender jar. Brown the almonds and the stale tortilla in the same oil (add more if necessary) and transfer to the blender jar. Add the bread. Now blend this mixture to a smooth paste, adding a little vegetable stock if necessary. Add this mixture to the chilli paste and stir together well.

5 Sauté the chilli mixture over medium heat for 5 minutes, stirring all the while. Add a little more oil if the mole sticks to the pan. Break the chocolate into small pieces and stir into the mixture. Continue to sauté, stirring occasionally, for 10 more minutes.

6 Now stir in the vegetable stock or bouillon and continue to cook, stirring from time to time, for about 40 minutes or longer if necessary. If the mixture seems too thick add a little stock or water. If it is spluttering too much, partially cover with a lid. It should be thick and should coat both sides of a wooden spoon, but liquid enough to call a sauce. Add sea salt to taste and remove from the heat. This will hold for 2 to 3 days in the refrigerator and can be frozen.

Cheese Enchiladas with Mole Sauce

Serves 6.

Imperial (Metric)	American
18 corn tortillas	18 corn tortillas
3 to 4 tablespoons safflower, corn or vegetable oil	3 to 4 tablespoons safflower, corn or vegetable oil
½ teaspoon chilli powder	½ teaspoon chili powder
½ teaspoon ground cumin	½ teaspoon ground cumin
Sea salt to taste	Sea salt to taste
1 small tin tomato purée	1 small can tomato sauce
¾ lb (340g) mild Cheddar cheese	¾ pound mild Cheddar or Monterey Jack cheese
1 small onion, minced	1 small onion, minced
1 recipe Mole Sauce (page 187)	1 recipe Mole Sauce (page 187)
3 tablespoons toasted sesame seeds	3 tablespoons toasted sesame seeds

1 Preheat the oven to 350 degrees F (180°C, gas mark 4). Oil a 3-pint (2 litre/2-quart) baking dish.

2 Heat 2 tablespoons of the oil in a large, heavy-bottomed frying pan. Combine the spices and sea salt and add a generous pinch to the oil. Add 2 to 3 tablespoons of tomato sauce and stir together. Sauté the tortillas on each side, just until flexible, being careful not to crisp, and drain on paper towels.

3 Sprinkle 2 to 3 tablespoons of cheese and a smattering of onion on each tortilla and roll up. Place in a neat line in the baking dish (you may have to do 2 layers). Cover with foil and place in the preheated oven. Bake 30 minutes, or until the cheese is bubbling.

4 Meanwhile heat the mole sauce on the top of the stove. If the sauce is too thick, thin out with water or vegetable stock. When the enchiladas are ready, spoon the sauce over the enchiladas, sprinkle with sesame seeds and serve at once. You can also arrange two to three enchiladas on individual plates, top with the sauce, sprinkle with sesame seeds and serve.

Potato and Avocado Tacos with Green Salsa

12 tacos.

Imperial (Metric)	American
1 lb (500g) new or boiling potatoes, diced	1 pound new or boiling potatoes, diced
3 to 4 tablespoons safflower oil	3 to 4 tablespoons safflower oil
1 small onion, thinly sliced	1 small onion, thinly sliced
½ teaspoon ground cumin	½ teaspoon ground cumin
½ teaspoon chilli powder	½ teaspoon chili powder
2 ripe avocados, diced and tossed with 1 tablespoon lemon juice	2 ripe avocados, diced and tossed with 1 tablespoon lemon juice
Sea salt to taste	Sea salt to taste
¼ lb (115g) mild Cheddar cheese, grated	¼ pound mild Cheddar or Monterey Jack cheese, grated
12 corn tortillas	12 corn tortillas
1 recipe Green Tomato Sauce (page 174)	1 recipe Green Tomato Sauce (page 174)

1 Steam the potatoes until crisp-tender, about 10 minutes.

2 Heat 1 tablespoon of the safflower oil in a heavy-bottomed frying pan and sauté the onion until tender. Add cumin, chilli powder and the potatoes and continue to sauté until the vegetables are just beginning to brown, about 10 minutes. Add more oil if necessary.

3 Remove the onions and potatoes from the heat and toss with the avocados. Add sea salt to taste.

4 Heat the tortillas until flexible in a dry frying pan. Place two heaped tablespoons of the potato-avocado mixture on each tortilla, and top with a spoonful of Green Salsa and a sprinkling of grated cheese. Roll up like an enchilada, or fold in half.

5 Heat the remaining oil in the frying pan and sauté the tacos on both or all sides (depending on whether they are rolled or folded) just until crisp. Serve at once, topping each taco with additional Green Salsa.

7. Salads and Dressings

Curry Mayonnaise

10 fl oz (285ml/1¼ cups).

Imperial (Metric)	American
1 egg	1 egg
2 teaspoons red wine or cider vinegar	2 teaspoons red wine or cider vinegar
½ to ¾ teaspoon sea salt, to taste	½ to ¾ teaspoon sea salt, to taste
1 teaspoon Dijon mustard	1 teaspoon Dijon mustard
¼ teaspoon freshly ground pepper	¼ teaspoon freshly ground pepper
2 teaspoons curry powder	2 teaspoons curry powder
¼ teaspoon chilli powder	¼ teaspoon chili powder
¼ teaspoon turmeric	¼ teaspoon turmeric
8 fl oz (225ml) safflower or vegetable oil	1 cup safflower or vegetable oil
2 tablespoons lemon juice, or to taste	2 tablespoons lemon juice, or to taste
Up to 1 teaspoon mild-flavoured honey (optional)	Up to 1 teaspoon mild-flavored honey (optional)

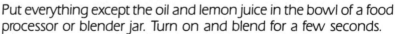

1 Put everything except the oil and lemon juice in the bowl of a food processor or blender jar. Turn on and blend for a few seconds.

2 With the food processor or blender still running, add the oil in a very slow stream, practically a drop at a time. If you are using a blender you may have to stop and stir the mixture from time to time. When all the oil has been added, add the lemon juice. Taste and adjust seasonings, adding salt, lemon juice or curry powder to taste. If you want the mayonnaise slightly sweet, add up to 1 teaspoon honey.

Curried Yogurt Dressing

12 fl oz (300ml/1½ cups).

Imperial (Metric)	American
Juice of 2 lemons	Juice of 2 lemons
8 fl oz (225ml) natural low-fat yogurt	1 cup plain low-fat yogurt
3 tablespoons mayonnaise	3 tablespoons mayonnaise
1 teaspoon Dijon-style mustard	1 teaspoon Dijon-style mustard
½ teaspoon turmeric	½ teaspoon turmeric
½ teaspoon chilli powder	½ teaspoon chilli powder
½ teaspoon freshly grated ginger	½ teaspoon freshly grated ginger
½ teaspoon paprika	½ teaspoon paprika
2 teaspoons curry powder	2 teaspoons curry powder
Pinch of cayenne	Pinch of cayenne
Sea salt and freshly ground pepper to taste	Sea salt and freshly ground pepper to taste

Blend all the ingredients together and refrigerate until ready to use.

Lemon-Curry Vinaigrette

6 fl oz (200ml/¾ cup).

Imperial (Metric)	American
2 fl oz (60ml) lemon juice	¼ cup lemon juice
1 teaspoon Dijon mustard	1 teaspoon Dijon mustard
½ teaspoon cumin	½ teaspoon cumin
¼ teaspoon curry powder	¼ teaspoon curry powder
Pinch of sea salt	Pinch of sea salt
¼ teaspoon soya sauce	¼ teaspoon soy sauce
4 fl oz (120ml) safflower oil	½ cup safflower oil
A generous amount of freshly ground pepper	A generous amount of freshly ground pepper

Combine the lemon juice, mustard, cumin, curry powder, sea salt and soya (soy) sauce and stir together well. Whisk in the oil and blend thoroughly. Add lots of freshly ground pepper.

Honey-Lemon Salad Dressing

6 fl oz (200ml/¾ cup).

Imperial (Metric)	American
2 fl oz (60ml) lemon juice	¼ cup lemon juice
1 tablespoon mild-flavoured honey	1 tablespoon mild-flavoured honey
1 teaspoon Dijon mustard	1 teaspoon Dijon mustard
Freshly ground pepper to taste	Freshly ground pepper to taste
¼ teaspoon ground ginger, or ½ to ¾ teaspoon grated fresh ginger, to taste	¼ teaspoon ground ginger, or ½ to ¾ teaspoon grated fresh ginger, to taste
¼ teaspoon soya sauce	¼ teaspoon soy sauce
4 fl oz (120ml) safflower oil	½ cup safflower oil

Combine the lemon juice, honey, mustard, pepper, ginger and soya (soy) sauce and stir together well. Whisk in the oil and blend thoroughly.

Moroccan Carrot Salad

Serves 4 to 6.

Imperial (Metric)	American
1 lb (500g) carrots, peeled and grated	1 pound carrots, peeled and grated
¾ oz (20g) minced fresh parsley	¾ cup minced fresh parsley
Pinch of sea salt	Pinch of sea salt
1 tablespoon orange flower water	1 tablespoon orange flower water
1½ teaspoons mild-flavoured honey	1½ teaspoons mild-flavored honey
Juice of 2 lemons	Juice of 2 lemons
¼ teaspoon allspice	¼ teaspoon allspice
½ teaspoon ground cumin	½ teaspoon ground cumin
Leaf lettuce for the platter or bowl	Leaf lettuce for the platter or bowl

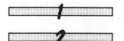 Combine the carrots, parsley and sea salt.

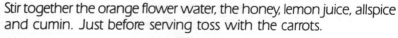 Stir together the orange flower water, the honey, lemon juice, allspice and cumin. Just before serving toss with the carrots.

 Line a platter or bowl with lettuce leaves, top with the carrots and serve.

Mexican Rice Salad

Serves 6 to 8.

Imperial (Metric)	American
For the Salad	For the Salad
½ lb (250g) brown rice	1 cup brown rice
¾ pint (500ml) water	2 cups water
½ teaspoon saffron	½ teaspoon saffron
Sea salt and freshly ground pepper to taste	Sea salt and freshly ground pepper to taste
½ lb (250g) green beans, trimmed and blanched	½ pound green beans, trimmed and blanched
1 red pepper, seeded and cut in thin strips	1 red pepper, seeded and cut in thin strips
4 spring onions, chopped	4 green onions, chopped
4 to 5 tablespoons pine nuts, to taste	4 to 5 tablespoons pine nuts, to taste
1 small cucumber, peeled, seeded and chopped	1 small cucumber, peeled, seeded and chopped
3 to 4 tablespoons chopped, fresh coriander, to taste	3 to 4 tablespoons chopped, fresh coriander, to taste
For the Dressing	For the Dressing
3 tablespoons wine or cider vinegar	3 tablespoons wine or cider vinegar
Juice of 1 large lemon	Juice of 1 large lemon
1 clove garlic, minced or put through a press	1 clove garlic, minced or put through a press
1 teaspoon Dijon-style mustard	1 teaspoon Dijon-style mustard
1 teaspoon ground cumin	1 teaspoon ground cumin
4 fl oz (120ml) safflower oil	½ cup safflower oil
2 fl oz (60ml) olive oil	¼ cup olive oil
Sea salt and freshly ground pepper to taste	Sea salt and freshly ground pepper to taste
Leaf lettuce for the bowl or platter (optional)	Leaf lettuce for the bowl or platter (optional)

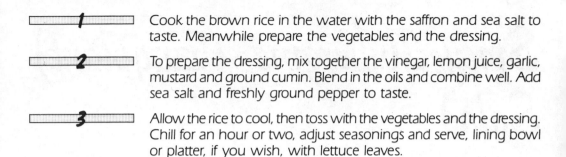

1. Cook the brown rice in the water with the saffron and sea salt to taste. Meanwhile prepare the vegetables and the dressing.

2. To prepare the dressing, mix together the vinegar, lemon juice, garlic, mustard and ground cumin. Blend in the oils and combine well. Add sea salt and freshly ground pepper to taste.

3. Allow the rice to cool, then toss with the vegetables and the dressing. Chill for an hour or two, adjust seasonings and serve, lining bowl or platter, if you wish, with lettuce leaves.

Moroccan Orange Salad

Serves 4.

Imperial (Metric)	American
1 tablespoon orange flower water	1 tablespoon orange flower water
⅛ to ¼ teaspoon cinnamon, to taste	⅛ to ¼ teaspoon cinnamon, to taste
1 teaspoon mild-flavoured honey	1 teaspoon mild-flavored honey
6 oranges, peels and zest removed, cut in thin slices	6 oranges, peels and zest removed, cut in thin slices
Pinch of nutmeg	Pinch of nutmeg
Fresh chopped mint for garnish	Fresh chopped mint for garnish
Pomegranate seeds for garnish	Pomegranate seeds for garnish

Combine the orange flower water, the cinnamon and honey and toss with the oranges. Sprinkle with a little nutmeg and chill, or serve at once, garnishing with fresh mint and pomegranate seeds.

Spicy Aubergine (Eggplant) Salad

Serves 4.

Imperial (Metric)	American
For the Salad	**For the Salad**
1 lb (500g) aubergine, peeled	1 pound eggplant, peeled
½ lb (250g) mangetout peas, trimmed	½ pound snow peas, trimmed
4 spring onions, sliced	4 green onions, sliced
1 tablespoon chopped fresh coriander	1 tablespoon chopped fresh coriander
For the Dressing	**For the Dressing**
2 to 3 tablespoons cider or white wine vinegar (to taste)	2 to 3 tablespoons cider or white wine vinegar (to taste)
1 clove garlic, minced or put through a press	1 clove garlic, minced or put through a press
1 teaspoon finely minced or grated fresh ginger	1 teaspoon finely minced or grated fresh ginger
1 tablespoon tamari soya sauce	1 tablespoon tamari soy sauce
2 tablespoons water	2 tablespoons water
½ teaspoon crushed dried hot pepper, or ⅛ to ¼ teaspoon cayenne, to taste	½ teaspoon crushed dried hot pepper, or ⅛ to ¼ teaspoon cayenne, to taste
4 tablespoons safflower or vegetable oil	4 tablespoons safflower or vegetable oil
2 tablespoons sesame oil	2 tablespoons sesame oil

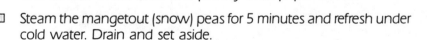

1 Cut the aubergine (eggplant) in strips about 2 inches (5cm) long, ½ inch (1cm) thick and 1 inch (2 cm) wide. Steam 15 minutes, or until tender. Drain, rinse and pat dry with paper towels.

2 Steam the mangetout (snow) peas for 5 minutes and refresh under cold water. Drain and set aside.

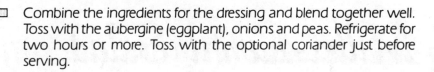 Combine the ingredients for the dressing and blend together well. Toss with the aubergine (eggplant), onions and peas. Refrigerate for two hours or more. Toss with the optional coriander just before serving.

Cold Minted Potatoes

Serves 6.

Imperial (Metric)	American
2 lb (1 kilo) red waxy or new potatoes	2 pounds red waxy or new potatoes
2 medium-sized cucumbers, or 1 long cucumber, peeled, seeded and diced	2 medium-sized cucumbers, or 1 long cucumber, peeled, seeded and diced
Sea salt to taste	Sea salt to taste
Juice of 2 lemons	Juice of 2 lemons
1 teaspoon ground roasted cumin (see page 14)	1 teaspoon ground roasted cumin (see page 14)
1 teaspoon ground roasted coriander (see page 14)	1 teaspoon ground roasted coriander (see page 14)
¼ teaspoon ground black pepper	¼ teaspoon ground black pepper
Pinch of cayenne, or to taste	Pinch of cayenne, or to taste
6 heaped tablespoons natural low-fat yogurt	6 heaping tablespoons plain low-fat yogurt
4 tablespoons chopped fresh mint	¼ cup chopped fresh mint

 Steam the potatoes until tender, about 20 minutes, and dice.

Toss the potatoes with the cucumber, sea salt, lemon juice, spices, yogurt and mint. Chill for at least one hour, and serve.

Note: This will keep for 3 to 4 days in the refrigerator.

Millet-Lentil Salad

Serves 4 to 6.

Imperial (Metric)	American
For the Dressing	**For the Dressing**
4 fl oz (120ml) lemon juice	**½ cup lemon juice**
1 clove garlic, minced or put through a press	**1 clove garlic, minced or put through a press**
2 teaspoons curry powder	**2 teaspoons curry powder**
½ teaspoon ground cumin	**½ teaspoon ground cumin**
¼ teaspoon ground coriander	**¼ teaspoon ground coriander**
1 teaspoon grated, fresh ginger	**1 teaspoon grated, fresh ginger**
Pinch of cayenne	**Pinch of cayenne**
Sea salt and freshly ground pepper, to taste	**Sea salt and freshly ground pepper, to taste**
8 fl oz (225ml) natural low-fat yogurt	**1 cup plain low-fat yogurt**
For the Salad	**For the Salad**
6 oz (170g) millet, cooked	**1 cup millet, cooked**
5 oz (140g) lentils, washed and cooked	**¾ cup lentils, washed and cooked**
½ lb (250g) carrots, peeled and thinly sliced	**½ pound carrots, peeled and thinly sliced**
4 to 6 spring onions, thinly sliced	**4 to 6 green onions, thinly sliced**
½ oz (15g) chopped fresh parsley	**½ cup chopped fresh parsley**
Lettuce leaves for garnish	**Lettuce leaves for garnish**

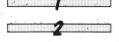

1 Mix together all the ingredients for the salad dressing and blend well.

2 Toss together the millet, lentils, carrots, green onions and parsley. Toss with the dressing, cover and chill for an hour or two. Serve over lettuce leaves.

Spicy Potato Salad with Coriander

Serves 6.

Imperial (Metric)	American
2 lb (1 kilo) red waxy or new potatoes	2 pounds red waxy or new potatoes
1 lb (500g) ripe tomatoes, diced	1 pound ripe tomatoes, diced
4 spring onions, minced	4 green onions, minced
1 clove garlic, minced or put through a press	1 clove garlic, minced or put through a press
1 teaspoon ground roasted cumin (see page 14)	1 teaspoon ground roasted cumin (see page 14)
Juice of 1 to 2 lemons, to taste	Juice of 1 to 2 lemons, to taste
Sea salt to taste	Sea salt to taste
Freshly ground pepper to taste	Freshly ground pepper to taste

 Steam the potatoes until tender, about 20 minutes.

Drain, refresh under cold water and toss with remaining ingredients. Chill at least one hour.

Note: This will keep 3 days in the refrigerator.

Curried Grains Salad

Serves 6 to 8.

Imperial (Metric)	American
1 recipe Curried Yogurt Dressing (page 193)	1 recipe Curried Yogurt Dressing (page 193)
8 oz (250g) raw brown rice, cooked	1 cup raw brown rice, cooked
8 oz (250g) raw wheat berries, cooked	1 cup raw wheat berries, cooked
4 oz (115g) raw chick peas, cooked	½ cup raw garbanzos, cooked
1 oz (30g) freshly grated Parmesan cheese	¼ cup freshly grated Parmesan cheese
1 medium-sized cucumber, peeled and chopped	1 medium-sized cucumber, peeled and chopped
1 green pepper, chopped	1 green pepper, chopped
1 oz (30g) lightly toasted peanuts (unsalted)	¼ cup lightly toasted peanuts (unsalted)
1 oz (30g) raisins	¼ cup raisins
1 apple, chopped	1 apple, chopped
¼ to ½ oz (7 to 15g) chopped fresh parsley	¼ to ½ cup chopped fresh parsley

For the Garnish	For the Garnish
1 head leaf lettuce	1 head leaf lettuce
2 tomatoes, cut in wedges	2 tomatoes, cut in wedges

1 Toss all the ingredients together with the dressing and chill for an hour or so.

2 Line a bowl or platter with lettuce leaves and top with the salad. Garnish with the tomatoes and serve.

Chichory (Endive), Apple and Mushroom Salad

Serves 4.

Imperial (Metric)	American
For the Salad	For the Salad
½ lb (250g) chicory, sliced in 1-inch (2cm) pieces	½ pound endive, sliced in 1-inch pieces
½ lb (250g) mushrooms, cleaned, trimmed and thinly sliced	½ pound mushrooms, cleaned, trimmed and thinly sliced
2 tart apples, cored and sliced	2 tart apples, cored and sliced
3 tablespoons chopped walnuts	3 tablespoons chopped walnuts
1 tablespoon chopped fresh chives	1 tablespoon chopped fresh chives
3 tablespoons minced fresh parsley	3 tablespoons minced fresh parsley
For the Dressing	For the Dressing
Juice of 1 lemon	Juice of 1 lemon
½ teaspoon Dijon mustard	½ teaspoon Dijon mustard
½ teaspoon mild-flavoured honey	½ teaspoon mild-flavored honey
4 fl oz (120ml) natural low-fat yogurt	½ cup plain low-fat yogurt
¾ teaspoon curry powder	¾ teaspoon curry powder
¼ teaspoon ground cumin	¼ teaspoon ground cumin

1   Toss together all the ingredients for the salad.

2   Mix together the ingredients for the dressing and blend well. Toss with the salad and serve.

Spicy Noodles Salad

Serves 6.

Imperial (Metric)	American
For the Dressing	**For the Dressing**
2 tablespoons crunchy unsalted peanut butter	**2 tablespoons crunchy unsalted peanut butter**
1 tablespoon soya sauce	**1 tablespoon soy sauce**
3 tablespoons white wine or cider vinegar	**3 tablespoons white wine or cider vinegar**
1 tablespoon Hot Chinese Pepper Oil (page 211)	**1 tablespoon Hot Chinese Pepper Oil (page 211)**
2 tablespoons sesame oil	**2 tablespoons sesame oil**
1 tablespoon minced fresh ginger	**1 tablespoon minced fresh ginger**
1 clove garlic, minced or put through a press	**1 clove garlic, minced or put through a press**
6 fl oz (200ml) Vegetable Stock (page 59) or Bouillon	**¾ cup Vegetable Stock (page 59) or Bouillon**
For the Salad	**For the Salad**
½ lb (250g) wholemeal or buckwheat noodles	**½ pound whole wheat or buckwheat noodles**
2 tablespoons sesame oil	**2 tablespoons sesame oil**
4 spring onions, sliced thin	**4 green onions, sliced thin**
3 tablespoons chopped fresh coriander	**3 tablespoons chopped fresh coriander**
Lettuce leaves for garnish	**Lettuce leaves for garnish**

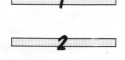 Blend together all the ingredients for the dressing in a blender until smooth.

2 Bring a large pot of water to a boil, add a teaspoon of sea salt and the noodles. Cook until al dente, 4 to 10 minutes, depending on the kind of noodle, drain and refresh under cold water. Toss at once with the sesame oil, spring (green) onions and coriander. Toss again with the dressing and correct seasonings, adding soya (soy) sauce, salt, pepper or cayenne if you wish. Line a platter with lettuce leaves

and top with the noodles. Chill and serve, or serve at once.

Note: The ginger-flavoured buckwheat noodles on page 156 would be particularly good here.

Spiced Carrot Salad

Serves 4 to 6.

Imperial (Metric)	American
2 lb (1 kilo) carrots, peeled and grated	**2 pounds carrots, peeled and grated**
3 tablespoons grated onion	**3 tablespoons grated onion**
Juice of 1 large lemon	**Juice of 1 large lemon**
1 teaspoon Dijon mustard	**1 teaspoon Dijon mustard**
2 teaspoons curry powder	**2 teaspoons curry powder**
½ teaspoon ground cumin	**½ teaspoon ground cumin**
½ teaspoon chilli powder	**½ teaspoon chili powder**
¼ teaspoon ground allspice	**¼ teaspoon ground allspice**
Pinch of cayenne	**Pinch of cayenne**
Sea salt and freshly ground pepper to taste	**Sea salt and freshly ground pepper to taste**
4 tablespoons safflower oil	**¼ cup safflower oil**
3 tablespoons natural low-fat yogurt	**3 tablespoons plain low-fat yogurt**
2 tablespoons chopped fresh coriander or parsley	**2 tablespoons chopped fresh coriander or parsley**

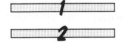 Toss together the carrots and grated onion.

Mix together the lemon juice, mustard, spices, salt, pepper, safflower oil and yogurt. Combine well and toss with the grated carrots. Correct seasonings, adding more spices if you wish. Sprinkle the chopped fresh coriander or parsley over the top and serve, or chill and serve.

Oriental Cucumber Salad

Serves 4.

Imperial (Metric)	American
3 tablespoons white wine or cider vinegar	3 tablespoons white wine or cider vinegar
1 tablespoon soya sauce	1 tablespoon soy sauce
2 teaspoons mild-flavoured honey	2 teaspoons mild-flavored honey
1 small clove garlic, minced or put through a press	1 small clove garlic, minced or put through a press
1 teaspoon minced fresh ginger	1 teaspoon minced fresh ginger
1/8 to 1/4 teaspoon cayenne or hot red pepper flakes	1/8 to 1/4 teaspoon cayenne or hot red pepper flakes
Freshly ground pepper to taste	Freshly ground pepper to taste
2 tablespoons sesame oil	2 tablespoons sesame oil
4 tablespoons safflower oil	4 tablespoons safflower oil
2 large cucumbers, peeled and sliced thin	2 large cucumbers, peeled and sliced thin
3 spring onions, green part and white, sliced thin	3 green onions, green part and white, sliced thin
2 tablespoons chopped fresh coriander	2 tablespoons chopped fresh coriander

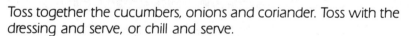 Mix together the vinegar, soya (soy) sauce, honey, garlic, ginger and cayenne. Add freshly ground pepper to taste and whisk in the sesame oil and safflower oil. Correct seasonings.

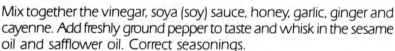 Toss together the cucumbers, onions and coriander. Toss with the dressing and serve, or chill and serve.

Cauliflower and Fresh Pea Salad

Serves 4 to 6.

Imperial (Metric)	American
1 lb (500g) cauliflower (about ½ head), broken into florets and sliced ½-inch (1cm) thick	1 pound cauliflower (about ½ head), broken into florets and sliced ½-inch thick
6 oz (170g) fresh peas	1 cup fresh peas
Juice of ½ to 1 lemon, to taste	Juice of ½ to 1 lemon, to taste
¾ pint (500ml) natural low-fat yogurt	2 cups plain low-fat yogurt
1 clove garlic, minced or put through a press	1 clove garlic, minced or put through a press
1 teaspoon Dijon mustard (optional)	1 teaspoon Dijon mustard (optional)
½ teaspoon ground roasted cumin seeds (more to taste)	½ teaspoon ground roasted cumin seeds (more to taste)
Sea salt and freshly ground pepper to taste	Sea salt and freshly ground pepper to taste
Cayenne pepper to taste	Cayenne pepper to taste
2 tablespoons chopped fresh coriander, mint or chives (optional)	2 tablespoons chopped fresh coriander, mint or chives (optional)

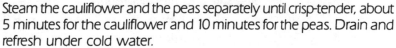

1 Steam the cauliflower and the peas separately until crisp-tender, about 5 minutes for the cauliflower and 10 minutes for the peas. Drain and refresh under cold water.

2 Mix together the lemon juice, yogurt, garlic, optional mustard, cumin, sea salt and pepper and the cayenne. Toss with the cauliflower and peas. Chill until ready to serve. Toss with the optional coriander, mint or chives just before serving.

Watercress, Orange, Fennel and Tomato Salad

Serves 4.

Imperial (Metric)	American
4 oz (115g) watercress, trimmed, washed and dried	2 cups watercress, trimmed, washed and dried
1 bulb fennel, sliced very thin	1 bulb fennel, sliced very thin
2 oranges, peeled, white pith removed, sectioned	2 oranges, peeled, white pith removed, sectioned
2 large ripe tomatoes, cut in thin wedges	2 large ripe tomatoes, cut in thin wedges
1 tablespoon chopped fresh mint	1 tablespoon chopped fresh mint

For the Dressing	For the Dressing
Juice of 1 lemon	Juice of 1 lemon
½ teaspoon freshly grated ginger	½ teaspoon freshly grated ginger
½ teaspoon Dijon mustard	½ teaspoon Dijon mustard
6 fl oz (200ml) natural low-fat yogurt	¾ cup plain low-fat yogurt
1 teaspoon curry powder	1 teaspoon curry powder
¼ teaspoon ground cumin	¼ teaspoon ground cumin
Sea salt and freshly ground pepper to taste	Sea salt and freshly ground pepper to taste

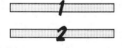 Toss together the watercress, fennel, oranges, tomatoes and mint.

Mix together the ingredients for the dressing and blend well. Toss with the salad just before serving.

Indian Peach Salad

Serves 6.

Imperial (Metric)	American
1 tablespoon honey	1 tablespoon honey
3 tablespoons lemon or lime juice	3 tablespoons lemon or lime juice
¼ teaspoon sea salt	¼ teaspoon sea salt
Freshly ground pepper to taste	Freshly ground pepper to taste
1½ teaspoons ground roasted cumin	1½ teaspoons ground roasted cumin
⅛ teaspoon cayenne pepper	⅛ teaspoon cayenne pepper
2 lb (1 kilo) fresh peaches, peeled and sliced	2 pounds fresh peaches, peeled and sliced

Mix together the honey, lemon or lime juice, salt, pepper, cumin and cayenne. Toss this dressing with the peaches. Serve.

8. Seasonings, Dips, Chutneys and Beverages

North Indian Spice Mix

This tasty mixture, introduced to me by Madhur Jaffrey, makes a nice seasoning for raw vegetables and nuts.

Imperial (Metric)	American
2 tablespoons whole coriander seeds	2 tablespoons whole coriander seeds
1 tablespoon whole cumin	1 tablespoon whole cumin
3 tablespoons sesame seeds	3 tablespoons sesame seeds
2 tablespoons coarse or regular sea salt	2 tablespoons coarse or regular sea salt
¼ teaspoon cayenne	¼ teaspoon cayenne
¼ teaspoon black pepper	¼ teaspoon black pepper

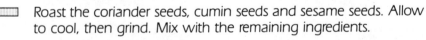

1 Roast the coriander seeds, cumin seeds and sesame seeds. Allow to cool, then grind. Mix with the remaining ingredients.

2 Sprinkle on raw vegetables or on peanuts or other nuts or seeds such as sunflower seeds or pumpkin seeds, which have first been sprinkled with a little lime juice.

Hot Chinese Pepper Oil

Use this for spicy Szechuan or Hunan dishes. It will keep for months in the refrigerator.

Imperial (Metric)	American
4 fl oz (120ml) safflower or vegetable oil	½ cup safflower or vegetable oil
1½ teaspoons ground hot dried red peppers (such as cayenne)	1½ teaspoons ground hot dried red peppers (such as cayenne)

 Place the oil in a pan and heat until it begins to ripple. Add the ground hot dried red peppers and remove from the heat.

 Allow to cool, then strain into a bottle. Store in the refrigerator. A teaspoon of this will add heat to any dish.

Pear-Apple Chutney

1½ pints (1 litre/1 quart).

Imperial (Metric)	American
1 lb (500g) apples, peeled, cored and chopped	1 pound apples, peeled, cored and chopped
2 lb (1 kilo) pears, peeled, cored and chopped	2 pounds pears, peeled, cored and chopped
1 tablespoon peeled and minced fresh ginger	1 tablespoon peeled and minced fresh ginger
8 fl oz (225ml) cider vinegar	1 cup cider vinegar
6 oz (175g) mild-flavoured honey	½ cup mild-flavored honey
1 small onion, minced	1 small onion, minced
3 cloves garlic, peeled and chopped	3 cloves garlic, peeled and chopped
1 small hot green chilli, seeded and minced	1 small hot green chilli, seeded and minced
4 tablespoons raisins	4 tablespoons raisins
1 teaspoon ground cardamom	1 teaspoon ground cardamom
½ teaspoon ground cloves	½ teaspoon ground cloves
1 tablespoon mustard seeds	1 tablespoon mustard seeds
½ teaspoon sea salt	½ teaspoon sea salt

1 Combine all the ingredients in a stainless steel or enamelled saucepan and bring to a boil. Reduce heat and simmer, uncovered, for one hour. Ladle into hot, sterilized jars, wipe the rims and seal with canning lids. Process in boiling water for 15 minutes. Cool.

2 Refrigerate once opened. Store unopened jars in a cool, dark place.

Carrot and Mustard Seed Relish

Serves 4 to 6.

Imperial (Metric)	American
1 lb (500g) carrots, peeled and grated	1 pound carrots, peeled and grated
2 tablespoons safflower or vegetable oil	2 tablespoons safflower or vegetable oil
½ teaspoon black mustard seeds	½ teaspoon black mustard seeds
1 or 2 hot green chillies, seeded and sliced (optional)	1 or 2 hot green chillies, seeded and sliced (optional)
1 tablespoon chopped fresh coriander	1 tablespoon chopped fresh coriander
Juice of 1 to 2 lemons, to taste	Juice of 1 to 2 lemons, to taste
Sea salt to taste	Sea salt to taste

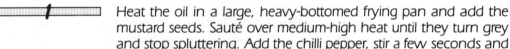

Heat the oil in a large, heavy-bottomed frying pan and add the mustard seeds. Sauté over medium-high heat until they turn grey and stop spluttering. Add the chilli pepper, stir a few seconds and toss with the carrots in a bowl.

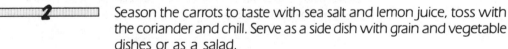

Season the carrots to taste with sea salt and lemon juice, toss with the coriander and chill. Serve as a side dish with grain and vegetable dishes or as a salad.

Sweet and Spicy Coriander Sauce

Makes 11 fl oz (230ml/1⅓ cups).

This intriguing sauce could be used as a dip for crudités, or spread on bread, or used as a sauce for vegetables. You could thin it out with more oil, or water from the prunes, for a thinner sauce for grains or pasta. It will keep for several days in the refrigerator.

Imperial (Metric)	American
6 pitted prunes	6 pitted prunes
1 oz (30g) fresh coriander leaves	1 cup fresh coriander leaves, tightly packed
½ oz (15g) chopped, fresh parsley	½ cup chopped, fresh parsley
2 fl oz (60ml) fresh lime juice	¼ cup fresh lime juice
2 cloves garlic, peeled	2 cloves garlic, peeled
½ teaspoon chopped fresh ginger	½ teaspoon chopped fresh ginger
¼ teaspoon sea salt	¼ teaspoon sea salt
¼ teaspoon freshly ground pepper	¼ teaspoon freshly ground pepper
4 tablespoons sesame tahini	¼ cup sesame tahini
2 to 4 tablespoons olive or safflower oil	2 to 4 tablespoons olive or safflower oil

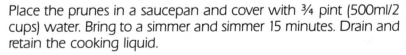

Place the prunes in a saucepan and cover with ¾ pint (500ml/2 cups) water. Bring to a simmer and simmer 15 minutes. Drain and retain the cooking liquid.

Combine all the ingredients except the oil and prune water in a blender or food processor fitted with the steel blade and blend together until you have a paste. Without stopping the blender or food processor, blend in the oil and enough of the prune water to give it the consistency you desire. This will depend on whether you wish to use the sauce as a dip, spread or sauce. The amount of oil or prune water you add will also depend on the consistency of your tahini. If it is very runny, you will need less oil, but if it is thick like peanut butter you will need more liquid.

 **3** Store the sauce in a covered jar in the refrigerator.

Mint and Coriander Dip or Chutney

½ pint (500ml/1¼ cups).

Imperial (Metric)	American
¾ oz (20g) fresh coriander leaves	¾ cup fresh coriander leaves
½ oz (15g) fresh mint leaves	½ cup fresh mint leaves
3 tablespoons water	3 tablespoons water
6 fl oz (200ml) natural low-fat yogurt	¾ cup plain low-fat yogurt
1 small hot green chilli, seeded and minced	1 small hot green chilli, seeded and minced
1 tablespoon lemon juice	1 tablespoon lemon juice
½ teaspoon mild-flavoured honey	½ teaspoon mild-flavored honey
Sea salt to taste	Sea salt to taste

 **1** Blend together the coriander and mint with the water in a blender or food processor.

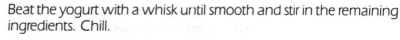 **2** Beat the yogurt with a whisk until smooth and stir in the remaining ingredients. Chill.

Ginger Tea

Serves 4.

This infusion is very strong, and you can temper it with added water and/or honey.

Imperial (Metric)	American
2-inch (5cm) piece fresh ginger root, peeled and chopped	2-inch piece fresh ginger root, peeled and chopped
3 tablespoons mild-flavoured honey (more to taste)	3 tablespoons mild-flavored honey (more to taste)
1½ pints (1 litre) water	4 cups water
1 stick cinnamon	1 stick cinnamon
4 cloves	4 cloves

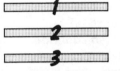 Combine all the ingredients in a saucepan and bring to a boil.

Reduce heat, cover and simmer 30 minutes.

Strain, correct sweetening and serve, or chill and serve. Dilute with water if too strong.

Iced Ginger-Lime Tea

Serves 2

Imperial (Metric)	American
¾ pint (500ml) water	2 cups water
1-inch (2cm) piece fresh ginger root, peeled and chopped	1-inch piece fresh ginger root, peeled and chopped
2 tablespoons mild-flavoured honey (more to taste)	2 tablespoons mild-flavored honey (more to taste)
4 fl oz (120ml) lime or lemon juice	½ cup lime or lemon juice
Ice cubes	Ice cubes

Combine the water, honey and ginger in a saucepan and bring to a simmer. Simmer 15 minutes and strain. Add the lime or lemon juice. Correct sweetening. Fill glasses with ice cubes and pour in the tea. Or chill the ginger-water infusion and combine with the lemon or lime juice just before serving.

Thandai (Indian Summer Punch)

Serves 4.

This is a rather exotic drink that is very popular in India.

Imperial (Metric)	American
2 oz (55g) blanched almonds	½ cup blanched almonds
1 tablespoon fennel seeds	1 tablespoon fennel seeds
Seeds from 4 cardamom pods	Seeds from 4 cardamom pods
3 cloves	3 cloves
3 tablespoons mild-flavoured honey	3 tablespoons mild-flavored honey
¾ pint (500ml) milk or water	2 cups milk or water

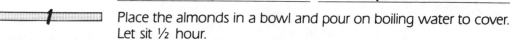 Place the almonds in a bowl and pour on boiling water to cover. Let sit ½ hour.

2 Grind all the spices together to a fine powder.

3 Combine the almonds, spices, honey and 8 fl oz (225ml/1 cup) of boiling water in a blender. Blend until thoroughly smooth, and pour into a bowl. Add another 4 fl oz (120ml/½ cup) of water to the blender and turn on to clean the blades and sides. Add to the mixture in the bowl. Strain this through cheesecloth, and chill overnight or for several hours.

4 Combine equal parts of the chilled mixture with milk (ice water may be subtituted). Serve very cold.

Spiced Minty Yogurt Drink

Serves 2.

Imperial (Metric)	American
8 fl oz (225ml) yogurt or buttermilk	1 cup yogurt or buttermilk
4 fl oz (120ml) water	½ cup water
12 mint leaves	12 mint leaves
½ teaspoon cumin	½ teaspoon cumin
8 ice cubes	8 ice cubes
Whole fresh mint leaves for garnish	Whole fresh mint leaves for garnish

1 Blend together all the ingredients except the ice cubes and whole mint leaves for the garnish until smooth in a blender.

2 Add the ice cubes and continue to blend another 20 to 30 seconds. Pour into glasses and garnish with the mint leaves. Serve.

Spiced Indian Tea

Serves 4 to 6.

Imperial (Metric)	American
2 tablespoons dark tea leaves, such as Darjeeling, Assam or Ceylon	2 tablespoons dark tea leaves, such as Darjeeling, Assam or Ceylon
8 white or green cardamom pods	8 white or green cardamom pods
A 2-inch (5cm) stick cinnamon	A 2-inch stick cinnamon
4 whole cloves	4 whole cloves
2 pints (1.25 litres) water	5 cups water
Honey or milk, to taste	Honey or milk, to taste

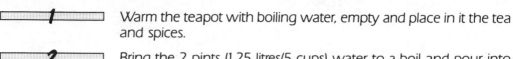 Warm the teapot with boiling water, empty and place in it the tea and spices.

2 Bring the 2 pints (1.25 litres/5 cups) water to a boil and pour into the teapot. Let steep 5 minutes, stir and serve, adding honey and/or hot milk to taste.

Apple Smoothie

Serves 2

Imperial (Metric)	American
8 fl oz (225ml) natural low-fat yogurt	1 cup plain low-fat yogurt
8 fl oz (225ml) apple juice	1 cup apple juice
2 apples, cored and chopped	2 apples, cored and chopped
1 teaspoon cinnamon	1 teaspoon cinnamon
½ teaspoon nutmeg	½ teaspoon nutmeg
1 teaspoon vanilla	1 teaspoon vanilla
1 banana, peeled, coarsely chopped	1 banana, peeled, coarsely chopped
2 teaspoons mild-flavoured honey	2 teaspoons mild-flavored honey
6 ice cubes	6 ice cubes

Blend all the ingredients together in a blender until smooth and frothy. Serve.

9. Desserts

Tofu Cheesecake

Serves 8.

Imperial (Metric)	American
For the Base	For the Crust
2 oz (55g) granola or muesli	½ cup granola
2 oz (55g) wheat germ (or use all granola)	½ cup wheat germ (or use all granola)
1 teaspoon cinnamon	1 teaspoon cinnamon
2 tablespoons melted butter	2 tablespoons melted butter
Additional butter for the pan	Additional butter for the pan

For the Filling	For the Filling
1½ lb (750g) tofu	1½ pounds tofu
8 fl oz (250ml) natural low-fat yogurt	1 cup plain low-fat yogurt
2 eggs	2 eggs
6 fl oz (170ml) mild-flavoured honey	¾ cup mild-flavored honey
Juice of 2 medium lemons	Juice of 2 medium lemons (⅓ cup lemon juice)
Grated rind of 1 lemon	Grated rind of 1 lemon
1 tablespoon vanilla	1 tablespoon vanilla
1 teaspoon nutmeg	1 teaspoon nutmeg
1 teaspoon cinnamon	1 teaspoon cinnamon
2 tablespoons sesame tahini	2 tablespoons sesame tahini
2 fl oz (60ml) Grand Marnier (optional)	¼ cup Grand Marnier (optional)
¼ teaspoon sea salt	¼ teaspoon sea salt
3 tablespoons wholemeal pastry flour	3 tablespoons whole wheat pastry flour

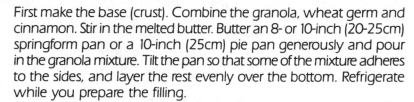

First make the base (crust). Combine the granola, wheat germ and cinnamon. Stir in the melted butter. Butter an 8- or 10-inch (20-25cm) springform pan or a 10-inch (25cm) pie pan generously and pour in the granola mixture. Tilt the pan so that some of the mixture adheres to the sides, and layer the rest evenly over the bottom. Refrigerate while you prepare the filling.

Preheat the oven to 350 degrees F (180°C, gas mark 4).

Purée all the filling ingredients together in a blender or food processor fitted with the steel blade until completely smooth. Pour into the prepared pan and bake in the preheated oven for 50 to 60 minutes, or until just beginning to brown.

Turn off the heat and leave in the oven 30 minutes. Remove from the oven, cool and chill.

Tofu-Banana Cream Pie

Serves 8.

Imperial (Metric)	American
1 Granola or Muesli base (see Tofu Cheesecake, page 220)	1 Granola Piecrust (see Tofu Cheesecake, page 220)
1 lb (500g) tofu	1 pound tofu
12 fl oz (340ml) natural low-fat yogurt	1½ cups plain low-fat yogurt
3 oz (90ml) mild-flavoured honey	⅓ cup mild-flavored honey
2 teaspoons vanilla	2 teaspoons vanilla
1 teaspoon nutmeg	1 teaspoon nutmeg
¼ teaspoon sea salt	¼ teaspoon sea salt
3 tablespoons wholemeal pastry flour	3 tablespoons whole wheat pastry flour
2 eggs	2 eggs
3 medium or large bananas	3 medium or large bananas
Juice of 1 to 2 lemons, to taste	Juice of 1 to 2 lemons, to taste
1 additional tablespoon lemon juice	1 additional tablespoon lemon juice
5 oz (140g) fresh strawberries, for garnish (optional)	1 cup fresh strawberries, for garnish (optional)

1 Preheat the oven to 350 degrees F (180°C, gas mark 4). Prepare the Granola base (piecrust) as for Tofu Cheesecake, page 220.

2 Slice the bananas and toss in 1 tablespoon lemon juice. Set aside 8 slices for decorating the pie.

3 Liquify all the remaining filling ingredients, except the bananas which you have set aside and the strawberries, in a blender or food processor fitted with the steel blade. Make sure the mixture is completely smooth.

4 Pour the filling into the base (piecrust) and bake 30 minutes in the preheated oven. Turn off the heat and allow the pie to cool in the oven for 30 minutes. Remove from the oven, decorate the top with the banana slices you set aside and the optional strawberries. Cover and chill.

Gingerbread

8 servings.

Imperial (Metric)	American
3 eggs	3 eggs
4 fl oz (120ml) treacle	½ cup dark molasses
4 fl oz (120ml) mild-flavoured honey	½ cup mild-flavored honey
1 tablespoon ground ginger	1 tablespoon ground ginger
1 teaspoon cinnamon	1 teaspoon cinnamon
½ teaspoon allspice	½ teaspoon allspice
½ teaspoon nutmeg	½ teaspoon nutmeg
¼ teaspoon sea salt	¼ teaspoon sea salt
Grated zest of 1 orange	Grated zest of 1 orange
8 oz (250g) wholemeal pastry flour	2 cups whole wheat pastry flour
1 teaspoon bicarbonate of soda	1 teaspoon baking soda
3 oz (85g) unsalted butter, melted	3 ounces unsalted butter, melted
4 fl oz (120ml) natural low-fat yogurt or buttermilk	½ cup plain low-fat yogurt or buttermilk

1 Preheat the oven to 350 degrees F (180°C, gas mark 4). Butter and lightly flour an 8-inch (20cm) square baking pan.

2 Beat the eggs until light and frothy. Add the molasses and the honey and continue to beat for a minute or two. Beat in the spices, sea salt and orange zest.

3 Sift together the flours and bicarbonate of (baking) soda. Gradually add one cup to the batter, beating slowly. Add the butter and yogurt or buttermilk, then the remaining flour. Mix just until blended.

4 Pour into the prepared pan and bake in the preheated oven about 45 minutes, or until the gingerbread has shrunk from the sides of the pan and a tester inserted in the centre comes out clean. Remove from the oven and cool on a rack. Serve topped with whipped cream or yogurt.

Baked Apples

Serves 4.

Imperial (Metric)	American
4 tart apples	**4 tart apples**
4 fl oz (120ml) apple juice	**½ cup apple juice**
1 teaspoon cinnamon	**1 teaspoon cinnamon**
½ teaspoon freshly grated nutmeg	**½ teaspoon freshly grated nutmeg**
¼ teaspoon ground cloves	**¼ teaspoon ground cloves**
1 teaspoon unsalted butter	**1 teaspoon unsalted butter**
2 teaspoons vanilla extract	**2 teaspoons vanilla extract**
3 tablespoons raisins	**3 tablespoons raisins**
2 tablespoons sunflower seeds or flaked almonds	**2 tablespoons sunflower seeds or slivered almonds**
Natural low-fat yogurt for topping	**Plain low-fat yogurt for topping**

 Preheat the oven to 350 degrees F (180°C, gas mark 4). Lightly butter a baking dish.

 Cut a cone-shaped cavity into the stem end of each apple and spoon a tablespoon of apple juice into each one. Combine the spices and sprinkle into the cavities. Add ½ teaspoon vanilla extract, then fill each apple with the raisins and sunflower seeds or almonds. Top with ¼ teaspoon butter. Add the remaining apple juice to the pan.

 Bake in a preheated oven until tender, about 45 minutes, basting from time to time with the apple juice in the pan.

Apple Crisp

Serves 6.

Imperial (Metric)	American
6 tart apples	6 tart apples
Juice of 1 lemon	Juice of 1 lemon
2 tablespoons mild-flavoured honey	2 tablespoons mild-flavored honey
1 teaspoon cinnamon	1 teaspoon cinnamon
½ teaspoon nutmeg	½ teaspoon nutmeg
¼ teaspoon cloves	¼ teaspoon cloves
2 tablespoons sunflower seeds	2 tablespoons sunflower seeds
1 tablespoon cornflour dissolved in 2 tablespoons water	1 tablespoon cornstarch dissolved in 2 tablespoons water
2 teaspoons vanilla	2 teaspoons vanilla

For the Topping	For the Topping
6 oz (170g) rolled oats	1½ cups rolled oats
2 oz (55g) wholemeal flour	½ cup whole wheat flour
¼ teaspoon sea salt	¼ teaspoon sea salt
2 teaspoons cinnamon	2 teaspoons cinnamon
1 teaspoon allspice	1 teaspoon allspice
3 oz (85g) unsalted butter or safflower oil	6 tablespoons unsalted butter or safflower oil
6 tablespoons mild-flavoured honey	⅓ cup mild-flavored honey

1 Preheat the oven to 375 degrees F (190°C; gas mark 5). Oil or butter a 3-pint (2 litre/2-quart) baking dish.

2 Combine the apples, lemon juice, honey, cinnamon, nutmeg, cloves, sunflower seeds, cornflour (starch) dissolved in the water and the vanilla. Spread evenly in the prepared baking dish.

3 Using a food processor or in a bowl with a wooden spoon, mix together the ingredients for the topping and combine well. Spread evenly over the apple mixture.

4 Bake in the preheated oven for 30 to 45 minutes, or until the top is brown and crisp. Serve warm, topped with plain low-fat yogurt.

Apple Sauce

Serves 4 to 6.

Imperial (Metric)	American
6 tart apples, cored and chopped	6 tart apples, cored and chopped
4 fl oz (120ml) water or apple juice	½ cup water or apple juice
2 tablespoons mild-flavoured honey	2 tablespoons mild-flavored honey
1 teaspoon cinnamon	1 teaspoon cinnamon
½ teaspoon nutmeg	½ teaspoon nutmeg
¼ teaspoon ground cloves	¼ teaspoon ground cloves
¼ teaspoon allspice	¼ teaspoon allspice
Juice of 1 lemon	Juice of 1 lemon

 Combine all the ingredients in a saucepan and simmer together over low heat for 45 minutes to an hour, stirring from time to time with a wooden spoon, until the mixture is thoroughly softened.

Mash to a purée with the back of a spoon. Eat warm or chilled, plain, with yogurt or as a spread on toast. This also makes a nice snack.

Dried Fruit Compote with Yogurt

Serves 4 to 6

Imperial (Metric)	American
5 oz (140g) dried apricots	1 cup dried apricots
5 oz (140g) prunes	1 cup prunes
3 oz (85g) raisins	½ cup raisins
3 oz (85g) chopped dried pears or peaches	½ cup chopped dried pears or peaches
1 stick cinnamon	1 stick cinnamon
4 cloves	4 cloves
¾ pint (500ml) water	2 cups water
¾ pint (500ml) red wine	2 cups red wine
4 tablespoons mild-flavoured honey	4 tablespoons mild-flavored honey
Freshly grated nutmeg to taste	Freshly grated nutmeg to taste
8 fl oz (250ml) natural low-fat yogurt or whipped cream	1 cup plain low-fat yogurt or whipped cream

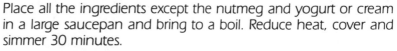 Place all the ingredients except the nutmeg and yogurt or cream in a large saucepan and bring to a boil. Reduce heat, cover and simmer 30 minutes.

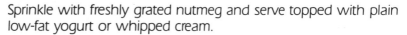 Sprinkle with freshly grated nutmeg and serve topped with plain low-fat yogurt or whipped cream.

Baked Pears

Serve 4 to 6

Imperial (Metric)	American
4 to 6 pears, peeled, cored and quartered	4 to 6 pears, peeled, cored and quartered
4 fl oz (120ml) apple juice	½ cup apple juice
¼ teaspoon cinnamon	¼ teaspoon cinnamon
¼ teaspoon freshly grated nutmeg	¼ teaspoon freshly grated nutmeg
Natural low-fat yogurt for topping (optional)	Plain low-fat yogurt for topping (optional)

 Preheat the oven to 350 degrees F (180°C, gas mark 4).

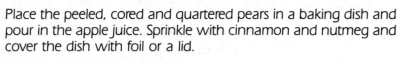 Place the peeled, cored and quartered pears in a baking dish and pour in the apple juice. Sprinkle with cinnamon and nutmeg and cover the dish with foil or a lid.

 Bake in the preheated oven for 30 minutes, or until the pears are soft but not mushy, and are aromatic. Serve hot or cool, with a spoonful or two of the apple juice. Top, if you wish, with plain low-fat yogurt.

Peaches in Red Wine

Serves 4 to 6

Imperial (Metric)	American
4 to 6 ripe peaches, peeled, pitted and sliced	4 to 6 ripe peaches, peeled, pitted and sliced
1¼ pints (750ml) red wine	3 cups red wine
4 tablespoons mild-flavoured honey	4 tablespoons mild-flavored honey
1 teaspoon cinnamon	1 teaspoon cinnamon

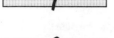

1 Blanch the peaches, run under cold water, and gently remove the skins.

2 Combine the wine, honey and cinnamon in a bowl. Slice the peaches and add to this mixture. Cover and chill. Serve cold.

Indian Pudding

Serves 6 to 8

This is adapted from my cookbook *The Vegetarian Feast.*

Imperial (Metric)	American
1½ pints (1 litre) milk, scalded	1 quart milk, scalded
6 tablespoons stone-ground yellow cornmeal	6 tablespoons stone-ground yellow cornmeal
6 level tablespoons treacle	⅓ cup molasses
3 tablespoons mild-flavoured honey	3 tablespoons mild-flavored honey
4 eggs, beaten	4 eggs, beaten
½ teaspoon sea salt	½ teaspoon sea salt
1 teaspoon ground ginger	1 teaspoon ground ginger
½ teaspoon freshly grated nutmeg	½ teaspoon freshly grated nutmeg
3 tablespoons butter	3 tablespoons butter
3 oz (85g) raisins	½ cup raisins

 Preheat the oven to 325 degrees F (170°C, gas mark 3). Butter a 3-pint (2 litre/2-quart) casserole or soufflé dish.

 Bring the milk to the boiling point in a 3- or 4-pint (2- or 3-litre/2- or 3-quart) saucepan. Pour in the cornmeal in a slow stream, stirring all the while with a wooden spoon as if you were making polenta. Bring to a gentle boil and cook over low heat, stirring, for about 15 minutes, or until the mixture is thick and creamy. Add the treacle (molasses) and honey and cook another 5 minutes.

 Remove from the heat and stir in the remaining ingredients. Mix well.

Pour the pudding into the prepared baking dish and bake for 1 to 1½ hours in the preheated oven, or until a knife comes out clean and the top is just beginning to brown.

Grapefruit and Figs with Ginger and Lime

Serves 4 to 6

Imperial (Metric)	American
8 fresh figs, quartered or cut in half	8 fresh figs, quartered or cut in half
3 pink grapefruit, peeled, white pith removed, and sectioned	3 pink grapefruit, peeled, white pith removed, and sectioned
6 level tablespoons lime juice	⅓ cup lime juice
4 tablespoons mild-flavoured honey	4 tablespoons mild-flavored honey
2 teaspoons minced fresh ginger	2 teaspoons minced fresh ginger
¼ teaspoon cinnamon	¼ teaspoon cinnamon

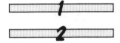 Toss together the figs and grapefruit.

2 Mix together the lime juice, honey, ginger and cinnamon. Toss with the fruit and serve, or chill and serve.

Cherry Clafouti

Serves 6

Imperial (Metric)	American
1½ lb (750g) pitted cherries	1½ pounds pitted cherries
10 fl oz (285ml) milk	1¼ cups milk
4 tablespoons mild-flavoured honey	4 tablespoons mild-flavored honey
3 eggs	3 eggs
1 tablespoon vanilla	1 tablespoon vanilla
¼ teaspoon nutmeg	¼ teaspoon nutmeg
Pinch of sea salt	Pinch of sea salt
6 level tablespoons unbleached white flour	⅓ cup unbleached white flour
6 level tablespoons wholemeal pastry flour	⅓ cup whole wheat pastry flour
2 tablespoons Kirsch	2 tablespoons Kirsch
Natural low-fat yogurt or cream for topping	Plain low-fat yogurt or cream for topping

 Pit the cherries and retain any liquid.

 Place the milk, the liquid from the cherries, honey, eggs, vanilla, nutmeg and salt in a blender and turn it on. Add the flours while the blender is running. Blend for 1 minute. If mixing by hand, blend together the eggs and flour with a wooden spoon and whisk or beat in the liquids. Strain through a fine strainer and stir in the kirsch. Let the batter rest for 30 minutes.

 Preheat the oven to 350 degrees F (180°C, gas mark 4). Butter a 3-pint (2 litre/2-quart) flameproof baking dish and pour in a ¼-inch (½cm) layer of batter. Place over moderate heat for 1 to 2 minutes, or just until a film has set on the bottom. Now spread the cherries in an even layer and pour on the remaining batter.

Place in the preheated oven and bake 45 minutes, or until puffed and brown and a knife plunged into the centre comes out clean. Serve hot or warm, with a little cream of yogurt to moisten.

Mangoes, Kiwi and Pineapple in Syrup

Serves 6 to 8

Imperial (Metric)	American
For the Syrup	For the Syrup
1½ pints (1 litre) water	1 quart water
4 fl oz (120ml) mild-flavoured honey	½ cup mild-flavored honey
1 clove	1 clove
½ teaspoon Chinese Five-spice powder	½ teaspoon Chinese Five-spice powder
Grated zests of 2 limes	Grated zests of 2 limes
Grated zest of 1 lemon	Grated zest of 1 lemon
1½ vanilla beans, split in half	1½ vanilla beans, split in half
1 teaspoon minced fresh ginger	1 teaspoon minced fresh ginger
3 coriander seeds	3 coriander seeds
1 sprig mint	1 sprig mint
For the Fruit	For the Fruit
2 large mangoes, peeled, seeded and diced	2 large mangoes, peeled, seeded and diced
½ fresh, ripe pineapple, peeled, cored and diced	½ fresh, ripe pineapple, peeled, cored and diced
8 kiwis, peeled and sliced	8 kiwis, peeled and sliced
1 tablespoon chopped fresh mint	1 tablespoon chopped fresh mint

1 First make the syrup. Combine all the ingredients in a large saucepan and bring to a boil. Remove from the heat and allow to cool. Cover and chill for several hours.

2 Place the fruit in a serving bowl. Strain in the syrup. Toss gently and cover. Refrigerate for at least two hours.

3 Just before serving toss with the mint.

Gingersnaps

4 to 5 dozen

Imperial (Metric)	American
6 oz (55g) butter	6 ounces butter
6 tablespoons mild-flavoured honey	6 tablespoons mild-flavored honey
4 fl oz (120ml) treacle	½ cup molasses
1 egg	1 egg
12 oz (340g) wholemeal pastry flour	2½ cups whole wheat pastry flour
¼ teaspoon sea salt	¼ teaspoon sea salt
1 teaspoon ground cinnamon	1 teaspoon ground cinnamon
¼ teaspoon freshly ground pepper	¼ teaspoon freshly ground pepper
1 tablespoon ground ginger	1 tablespoon ground ginger

1 Preheat the oven to 350 degrees F (180°C, gas mark 4). Butter baking sheets.

2 Cream together the butter, honey and treacle (molasses) and beat in the egg. Sift together the whole wheat pastry flour, sea salt, cinnamon, pepper and ground ginger. Add to the liquid ingredients and mix well.

3 Drop by scant tablespoons onto the baking sheets, about 2 inches apart. Take a glass or jar and dip the bottom into cool water, then press out the cookies very thin. Keep wetting the glass to avoid sticking.

4 Bake for 10 to 12 minutes; cool on racks.

Bibliography and Suggested Reading

Cost, Bruce, *Ginger, East to West*, Aris Books, Berkeley, Los Angeles, 1984.

David, Elizabeth, *Spices, Salt and Aromatics in the English Kitchen*, Penguin Books, London and New York, 1970.

David, Elizabeth, *English Bread and Yeast Cookery*, The Viking Press, London and New York, 1980.

Jaffrey, Madhur, *An Invitation to Indian Cooking*, Jonathan Cape, London, 1976.

Jaffrey, Madhur, *World of the East Vegetarian Cooking*, Alfred A. Knopf & Co., New York, 1981.

Kennedy, Diane, *The Cuisines of Mexico*, Harper & Row, Publishers, New York, 1972.

Rosengarten, Frederick Jr., *The Book of Spices*, Jove Publications, Inc., New York, 1973.

Sahni, Julie, *Classic Indian Cooking*, William Morrow & Co., Inc., New York, 1980.

Sax, Richard, *Cooking Great Meals Every Day*, Random House, New York, 1982.

Sax, Richard, *Old Fashioned Desserts*, Irena Chalmers Cookbooks, Inc., New York, 1984.

Scott, David, *Middle Eastern Vegetarian Cookery*, Rider & Co., Ltd, London, 1981.

Shulman, Martha Rose, *Herb and Honey Cookery*, Thorsons Publishers Ltd, Wellingborough and New York, 1984.

Stobart, Tom, *Herbs, Spices and Flavorings*, Penguin Books, London, 1977.

Tropp, Barbara, 'All About Peppercorns', in *Food and Wine*, May, 1985.

Index